TABLE OF

MW01491667

THE COMPLETE GUIDE TO AUSTRALIAN CATTLE DOGS

Tarah Schwartz

LP Media Inc. Publishing

Text copyright © 2019 by LP Media Inc.

www.lpmedia.org

Publication Data

Tarah Schwartz

The Complete Guide to Australian Cattle Dogs ---- First edition.

Summary: "Successfully raising a Australian Cattle Dog from puppy to old age" --- Provided by publisher.

ISBN: 978-1-71032-9-728

[1.Australian Cattle Dogs --- Non-Fiction] I. Title.

This book has been written with the published intent to provide accurate and authoritative information in regard to the subject matter included. While every reasonable precaution has been taken in preparation of this book the author and publisher expressly disclaim responsibility for any errors, omissions, or adverse effects arising from the use or application of the information contained inside. The techniques and suggestions are to be used at the reader's discretion and are not to be considered a substitute for professional veterinary care. If you suspect a medical problem with your dog, consult your veterinarian.

Design by Sorin Rădulescu

First paperback edition, 2019

CHAPTER 1
The Australian Cattle Dog

What Is an Australian Cattle Dog?

"The reason this breed is so loved by ACD enthusiasts is for their unique qualities. They are well known as being 'velcro' dogs, who quickly establish a bond with their owners and live to love them! They are highly intelligent and easy to train, despite their stubborn streaks. They typically handle discipline well and keep trying harder to please you, in most cases your praise is enough as reward for good behavior. Their greatest joy in life is to not leave your side, most love to go everywhere with you - car rides, in the boat, or 4 wheeler, anywhere they can fit! They are known also for their great ability to be versatile; they have been personal protection dogs, scent tracking, therapy, duck retrieving dogs, and many other uses among their traditional use as a herding dog - making them a uniquely utilitarian breed."

Kelsey Bolton
Flintlock Farms

Photo Courtesy of
Linda Multušová

Photo Courtesy of
Kim Langevin

Australian Cattle Dogs are compact, muscular herding dogs that originated in Australia. Originally bred to move cattle, they are resilient and intelligent dogs capable of driving cattle over long distances. As herders, they are intense, driven working dogs that have a bit of an independent streak. Australian Cattle Dogs are credited with having an enormous impact on the beef industry in Australia. Without the breed, moving cattle across the vast landscape of Australia would have been immensely difficult. Their athleticism has also helped the breed succeed in a variety of modern-day dog sports. As pets, Australian Cattle Dogs are affectionate and energetic companions.

Although the breed is most commonly referred to as the Australian Cattle Dog, the dogs are also sometimes called Red or Blue Heelers, Queensland Heelers, ACDs, or simply Cattle Dogs. Red or Blue Heelers typically reference the dogs' coloring as being either red or blue with white ticking. The name Queensland Heeler originally helped differentiate the dogs being bred in Queensland, Australia, from those being born in New South Wales. However, since Australian Cattle Dogs can now be found all over the world, the moniker Queensland Heeler is now nothing more than a nickname. As the most popular breed created to move cattle, the Australian Cattle Dog is often referred to as just the Cattle Dog.

The Australian Cattle Dog is a short-haired breed that requires relatively little grooming. The smooth double coat can be maintained with weekly

Photo Courtesy of
Petra Plank

brushing and an occasional bath. The breed is well-known for its distinctive coat colors. Although puppies are born white, they develop either blue or red coloring at around four weeks of age.

The Australian Cattle Dog was first recognized by the American Kennel Club (AKC) in 1980. After a brief period in the Miscellaneous class and Working Group, the breed was eventually assigned to the Herding Group. In terms of popularity, the AKC ranks the breed as 55 out of 193 recognized breeds. The breed is a popular choice among competitors in agility and obedience. In addition to their success as herders, Australian Cattle Dogs can also be found competing in dock diving, fly ball, and nose work. Their incredible intelligence and trainability make them ideal partners in any dog sport.

Australian Cattle Dogs are quite healthy, but there are a few genetic disorders that are common to the breed, including hip dysplasia, progressive retinal atrophy, and deafness. Breeders are actively working to eliminate these disorders from the breed. According to the AKC, most Australian Cattle Dogs have a life span of about 12 to 15 years.

History of the Australian Cattle Dog

In the 1840s, George Elliot of Queensland, Australia, was on a quest to create the ideal working breed. As the owner of multiple cattle stations, he recognized the difficulty in moving cattle across rugged terrain to the market in Sydney. He began crossing Collies with tamed Dingoes. Dingoes were used because of their stamina and ability to work independently. The offspring of these crosses were impressive workers, but fellow cattlemen Jack and Harry Bagust felt that they could still improve upon the breed. They crossed the dogs with Dalmatians to instill a love of horses, and Black and Tan Kelpies to improve the breed's work ethic. The Dalmatian added the breed's signature speckled coat, while the Black and Tan Kelpies are responsible for the dark masks and tan markings that can be found on the modern-day Australian Cattle Dog. The Bagusts only kept the puppies that they felt were closest to their ideal dog.

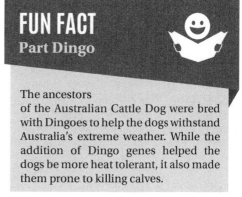

FUN FACT
Part Dingo

The ancestors of the Australian Cattle Dog were bred with Dingoes to help the dogs withstand Australia's extreme weather. While the addition of Dingo genes helped the dogs be more heat tolerant, it also made them prone to killing calves.

As word spread about the Bagusts' hardworking new breed, the breed became highly sought after by cattlemen and drovers across the country, with the

Photo Courtesy of Anthony Stankus

FUN FACT
Lots of Names

Australian Cattle Dogs go by many different names, including Blue Heeler, Red Heeler, Australian Heeler, and Queensland Heeler. The heeler name comes from the dogs' method of biting the heels of cattle to herd them.

blue-coated variety ultimately becoming more popular than the red. As cattlemen began to breed their own lines, the name Queensland Heeler was given to those dogs born in the state of Queensland. Although some breeders attempted to alter the breed further, it was done with relatively little success. So breeders chose instead to focus on the dogs' working ability and body type.

In 1893, a breeder named Robert Kaleski drew up the first breed standard for the Australian Cattle Dog. He based the standard on the body type of the Dingo, as he believed that this was the ideal shape for a dog suited to cross the harsh wilderness of Australia alongside cattle. In 1903, his standard was approved by the Cattle and Sheep Dog Club of Australia and the Kennel Club of New South Wales.

The Australian Cattle Dog's popularity continued to rise as it was exported to countries around the world. In May 1980, the breed was officially recognized by the AKC. By September 1980, the breed was placed in the Working Group, where it spent the next three years. The AKC's Herding Group was established in 1983, and the breed was placed alongside other herding breeds such as the Border Collie and German Shepherd. The Australian Cattle was officially recognized by the Canadian Kennel Club in 1980. By the end of that year, a dog by the name of Landmaster Carina became the first Australian Cattle Dog to officially earn both conformation and obedience titles. The first Australian Cattle Dogs arrived in the United Kingdom in 1980. By 1985, the Australian Cattle Dog Society had been formed and the breed was officially recognized by the Kennel Club of the United Kingdom.

The breed's affectionate nature makes it a popular choice for active families that can keep up with its high energy and intelligence. The breed also continues to excel at moving cattle and other livestock for farmers and ranchers around the world. Competitors in modern dog sports have also found success with the Australian Cattle Dog.

Physical Characteristics

Australian Cattle Dogs are medium-sized, weighing between 30 and 50 lbs. On average, males measure 17-20 inches at the withers and females measure 17-19 inches. Their overall appearance is that of a compact, muscular working dog. Dogs that do not appear to have great endurance or agility will be faulted in the show ring.

The breed standard describes the Australian Cattle Dog as having a broad skull with muscular jaws. The muzzle is of medium length and the nose is black. The eyes should be medium-sized, oval in shape, and dark brown in color. They should give the impression of high intelligence and alertness. The ears of the Australian Cattle Dog are of moderate size, and smaller ears are preferred over larger ears. They are set wide on the skull and should be moderately pointed, rather than rounded. The neck should be of medium length and extremely strong and muscular. Shoulders must be both muscular and well-angulated, sloping down to strong, parallel front legs. The Australian Cattle Dog's back should be level and the body should be only slightly longer than it is tall. The hindquarters are broad and muscular with straight, parallel hind legs. The feet should be round with short, well-arched toes. The tail is set moderately low and should rest in a slight curve.

The Australian Cattle Dog has a smooth double coat with a dense undercoat. The coat should be slightly longer along the neck, thighs, and tail, typically no longer than 1.5 inches in length. A coat that is too long or too short will be faulted in the show ring. The AKC only accepts two colors—red and blue. Blue-coated dogs should be blue or blue speckled and are accepted with or without black, blue, or tan markings on the head, legs, and throat. A blue dog may have a tan undercoat as long as it does not show through the outer coat. Any markings other than speckling or mottling are considered a fault. Red dogs should have an evenly speckled red coat, including their undercoat. The AKC allows for darker red markings on their head, as long as these are even.

Photo Courtesy of Bailey Miller

Breed Behavioral Characteristics

"This breed has the natural instinct to herd--they want to control movement. This means cattle, or anything else they are around, including people! They are an active, high drive dog by nature as well. Make certain you have a lifestyle that can provide plenty of mental and physical activity, training and socialization."

Gwen Shepperson
Buffalo Creek Cattle Dogs

One of the Australian Cattle Dog's most distinct characteristics is its intelligence. Renowned behaviorist Stanley Coren has rated the breed as the tenth most intelligent breed out of 138 breeds that he tested during his studies of canine intelligence. Coren claims that the breed needs fewer than five repetitions of a new command to understand what their handler is asking. He also suggests that the breed is likely to obey the first command 95% of the time or better. This intelligence makes the Australian Cattle Dog highly trainable, enabling it to succeed in a variety of dog sports and outdoor activities.

The Australian Cattle Dog is also known for its high energy. Due to its origins, the breed requires a significant amount of physical and mental stimulation. Without an adequate amount of stimulation, your Cattle Dog is likely to become frustrated and destructive.

Australian Cattle Dogs were bred to occasionally work independently of their humans. Although they needed to take commands and direction from their handlers, the breed also had to be able to make independent decisions in the moment when moving difficult livestock. As a result, the modern-day breed can be somewhat independent and requires strong and confident leadership. Australian Cattle Dogs can be stubborn, so training must be done in a way that keeps the dogs engaged and interested in the work. Without an assertive pack leader, Australian Cattle Dogs may feel the need to fill that role themselves, so it's important to remind the dog of your leadership both in training sessions and in the home.

The Australian Cattle Dog as a Working Dog

"Like any herding breed, but perhaps more so-ACDs, they were cre-ated for vigorous working conditions. Their drive and athleticism is too extreme for most homes unless they are given appropriate mental and physical outlets for their energy."

Brett Spader
Spader Kennels

Australian Cattle Dogs have strong herding instincts. In the presence of livestock, the dogs are calculated and deliberate. They can approach even the wildest stock with confidence. The breed was developed to work silent-ly, so it's uncommon and undesirable for Australian Cattle Dogs to bark ex-cessively while working. As "heelers," they move livestock by nipping at their heels. They may also nip at animals' heads if they need to stop or turn the stock. Instinctively, the breed understands that the proper technique is to nip at an animal's weight-bearing hind leg in order to dodge a kick from the other leg. These nips, known as "grips," are quick and are followed by an immediate release. With experience and training, working dogs will under-stand when force is necessary and when they can move animals using only their presence. Experienced working dogs will never use excessive or inap-propriate force with livestock.

Australian Cattle Dogs work as upright herders, meaning their posture tends to be more erect than many other herding breeds, such as Border Collies. Carrying their head at shoulder level, rather than in a crouched po-sition, enables Australian Cattle Dogs to keep a close eye on livestock while also allowing them to move quickly to bite or avoid being kicked. Although they work with an erect posture most of the time, crouching is required on occasion, especially with more challenging stock. The Australian Cattle Dog's innate herding instincts enable them to read the body language of livestock and respond accordingly with the correct posture and amount of force required to get the job done.

*Photo Courtesy of
Jesse du Pree*

Is an Australian Cattle Dog the Right Fit for You?

"Are you willing to have a PERMANENT sidekick? Heelers want to be with their humans at all times."

James C Beel
ACD Breeder

If you are looking for a working cattle dog to help you control livestock on your ranch or farm, the Australian Cattle Dog may be the ideal breed for you. However, if you want one as a family companion, you need to seriously consider whether you are able to provide the right environment for such an active and intelligent breed. This is not a breed that will be satisfied with a leisurely walk around the neighborhood once or twice a day. The Australian Cattle Dog is a high-energy breed that needs an adequate amount of exercise to prevent boredom and bad behavior.

Australian Cattle Dogs' herding instincts can cause problems if the dog attempts to herd small children by nipping them. As the owner of a herding dog, you must find ways to help your dog express his desire to herd without accidentally hurting anyone. You must be prepared to be a strong and assertive leader, teaching your dog that heeling family members is not appropriate. Firm and consistent training is essential throughout your dog's life, so you must be willing to dedicate yourself to your pet's training.

As self-appointed guardians of their livestock, Australian Cattle Dogs can be somewhat suspicious of strangers. Thus, socialization is particularly crucial to this breed, especially for family companions and sport dogs. It's unlikely that you'll be able to eliminate this trait from your dog, but with proper socialization your dog can learn how to interact with strangers appropriately. Introducing your dog to a variety of people, places, and animals will help give him the confidence he needs to safely accompany you wherever you go. Socialization requires a lot of time and effort, so you need to make sure that you're willing to make the commitment before deciding to bring home an Australian Cattle Dog.

CHAPTER 2
Choosing an Australian Cattle Dog

"First be honest with yourself about your expectations regarding dog ownership, and then look for an ACD with a temperament to match. A responsible breeder or rescue will be diligent in matching personalities."

Alison Whittington
Hardtack Australian Cattle Dogs

Buying vs. Adopting

Once you've decided on an Australian Cattle Dog as your ideal companion, you need to decide whether you'd rather buy a dog from a breeder or adopt from a shelter or rescue organization. Knowing what you want in a dog and picturing your long-term goals can help you decide where to get your new dog. Are you looking for a working ranch dog or a future show ring star? Is your new dog destined to be an active family companion or would you like to try out a few dog sports? If you have a good understanding of what you want from your Australian Cattle Dog, you'll be able to make an informed decision on whether adopting or buying is the right choice for you.

Photo Courtesy of Tory Farley

The first step in considering your ideal dog is to decide whether you would prefer to bring home a puppy or an adult dog. A puppy will require you to dedicate a lot of time and effort to training and supervision. It's a lot of work, but it can be a rewarding experience for the entire family. In addition, you'll need to house-train and properly socialize a puppy, which can be frustrating and time-consuming. Puppies may chew up your furniture or personal belongings. On the positive side, raising a puppy means you have the opportunity to train your dog however you want. You won't be working with bad habits from previous homes.

If you adopt an adult dog, it will already be past the frustrating puppy stages, including teething, and is likely to already be housetrained. Adult Austra-

FUN FACT
Cattle Dog History

The history of the Cattle Dog starts with blue merle Collie/Dingo mixes. They were excellent at herding cattle, but they needed to be mixed with other dogs to improve their personality. With the addition of Dalmatian and Kelpie genes, the Australian Cattle Dog developed into an excellent working breed.

lian Cattle Dogs may have a basic understanding of household manners and obedience, though this is never a guarantee. Remember, you can often find both puppies and adults at shelters and rescues and breeders may occasionally have retired breeding dogs or show dogs available.

You may also want to consider the gender of your future Australian Cattle Dog. This is especially important if you have other dogs at home. Some dogs may not get along with others of the same gender, so you may need to take your current dog's preferences and temperament into consideration. If you have no other pets, your new dog's gender may not matter to you, but at least you'll be able to discuss your options with the breeder or shelter staff.

The most important aspect to consider when picturing your ideal dog is its purpose. Knowing what you want to do with your new Australian Cattle Dog will have the biggest impact on where you find him or her. If you're looking for a working cattle dog, then you'll probably have the most success looking for a breeder with experience in this field. This is not to say that a rescued dog can't find success as a working dog, but you'll have a better chance of finding the dog of your dreams with the guidance of a reputable breeder. The same idea applies to show dogs and sport dogs. Rescue dogs are able to compete in a variety of AKC sports, so if you're interested in competition for fun, you may be fine competing with a dog adopted from a shelter. As for dogs who will primarily be family companions, you may not want to potentially spend thousands of dollars on the purchase of a pedigreed dog, so a shelter may be your best option. No matter what you intend to do with your dog, you should have some idea so that you can discuss your goals with the breeder or shelter staff.

How to Find a Reputable Breeder

"Do plenty of research on this breed to make certain it is a good fit for you, this is a very active and intelligent breed that requires a dedicated owner. Seek out breeders that are producing puppies from fully health tested dogs that are active in using their dogs for this breed's intended purpose, and raising puppies in an environment that will give them every opportunity to grow with health and confidence."

Gwen Shepperson
Buffalo Creek Cattle Dogs

Once you've decided to buy an Australian Cattle Dog from a breeder, you can begin searching for a reputable facility. It's important that you carefully research breeders in your area and not impulsively buy the first puppy you find. Finding a breeder who believes in improving the breed with every generation will give you a better chance at raising a healthy and well-adjusted dog. Good breeders will also be able to make recommendations based on their knowledge of their own dogs as well as your long-term goals.

Photo Courtesy of
Sharon Charlton

One of the best ways to find a reputable breeder is to ask others for recommendations. If you intend to show your Australian Cattle Dog, you may want to attend a few shows and ask some of the competitors about their dogs and which breeder they came from. If you're searching for a working stock dog, try asking a few local farmers or ranchers about their dogs. Not only will this give you the opportunity to get to know other breed enthusiasts, but it will give you an idea of the type of dog that these breeders are producing.

If you're unable to attend any local shows or talk to other owners or handlers, a simple internet search should yield more than a few results. Again, thorough research is essential. Many breeders update their websites regularly with their dogs' show records and upcoming or available litters. These websites will also have the breeders' contact information so you can get in touch with them. Once you find a breeder or two, you may want to do another search to see what kind of reputation they have. Just because they have a fancy website doesn't mean they're reputable.

Photo Courtesy of Afton Trout

Initially, you may want to contact more than one breeder. By discussing your needs with a few different breeders, you'll be better able to make an informed choice as to the best place to get your new dog. Remember, reputable breeders will be happy to discuss their dogs. They will readily produce all relevant health testing and performance records. If a breeder seems unwilling to discuss certain topics or is hesitant to produce health or performance documents, it may indicate that their dogs are not as high quality as they claim. Breeders who are dedicated to improving the breed will always be open and willing to talk about their dogs. They're more interested in finding the right home for their dogs than just selling them for the highest price. Most reputable breeders will encourage you to visit their home or kennel to meet their dogs. At certain times, they may limit visitors due to the presence of young, unvaccinated puppies in the home, but in such situations they are likely looking out for their dogs rather than trying to hide anything.

If you have any specific goals for your new dog, you will need to discuss them with the breeder. Finding a breeder that specializes in your chosen sport or type of work will allow you to choose a dog with the best potential to succeed. You'll be able to see the performance records for the parents and past litters and see if they have the temperament you're looking for. The breeder will also be able to help guide you through the process of choosing a puppy based on your needs and performance goals.

Health Tests and Certifications

"Dogs should be x-rayed and evaluated by OFA or PennHip for hip, el-bow, and patellar dysplasia with only passing score dogs used for breed-ing. All parent dogs, as well as puppies, should have a BAER Hearing Test to insure no deafness. Please seek out responsible breeders that have a program with health tested dogs to insure that your new puppy has the best opportunity to be healthy and durable throughout their lives."

Gwen Shepperson
Buffalo Creek Cattle Dogs

Reputable breeders regularly test their dogs for common genetic disor-ders in order to improve the health of the breed as a whole. By testing their dogs, they're able to make informed decisions on which dogs should and should not be bred. If a dog is tested and does not pass the test or is shown to be a carrier for a certain gene or trait, then the dog will be spayed or neu-tered to prevent it from passing the condition on to future generations.

The Orthopedic Foundation for Animals (OFA) is the leading American institution for canine genetic research. In addition to scientific research, the OFA runs a database containing the results of health tests for thousands of dogs of nearly every breed, including many not yet recognized by the AKC. Owners and breeders are able to have local veterinarians perform a variety of tests on their dogs and submit the results to the OFA. For a nominal fee, experts will examine the results, rate them, and make them publicly avail-able on the OFA website. For most tests, dogs must be over the age of 12 months, but certain tests have different age restrictions. The OFA website has a list of recommended tests for each breed as well as any specific re-quirements or restrictions.

The OFA requires Australian Cattle Dogs to undergo six different tests before their results can be posted on the website. Once all required test results are submitted, each dog is issued a unique Canine Health Informa-tion (CHIC) database number. There are also five other tests that are con-sidered optional. After the age of 24 months, Australian Cattle Dogs must be tested for hip dysplasia and elbow dysplasia. They must also be exam-ined by a veterinary ophthalmologist certified by the American College of Veterinary Ophthalmologists (ACVO). At any age, dogs must also be tested for congenital deafness and primary lens luxation, which is a disorder of the optical lens. A DNA test for Progressive Retinal Atrophy (PRA) is also required. Optional tests include examinations for patellar luxation and laxity in the joints that may result in future dysplasia, as well as hock x-rays. An advanced cardiac exam and further genetic testing for PRA is also optional but recommended.

Breeder Contracts and Guarantees

When you purchase a dog from a reputable breeder, you will probably need to sign a contract. This contract is intended to protect both you and the breeder financially while prioritizing the puppy's health and well-being. Generally, the contract specifies the exact puppy you will be taking home, the purchase price, and any conditions of the adoption. It may also specify what happens if either party violates any part of the agreement and what will happen to the puppy.

By signing the breeder's contract, you will be legally accepting the responsibility of caring for the puppy. Often, contracts stipulate when and if a puppy is to be spayed or neutered. Dogs competing in conformation can't be spayed or neutered. In the contract you will also agree to have the puppy immunized and dewormed as needed. Some breeders may also specify in their contracts what type of food you need to feed the dog. This is particularly true with breeders who feed their dogs raw diets, as they often want the puppy to continue with a similar diet.

The contract should also include a few statements regarding the health of the puppy at the time of purchase and what steps the breeder has taken to ensure the puppy's health up to that point. There may be certain guarantees against genetic disorders or diseases as well. There should also be a clause as to what happens if a puppy is found to have contracted a communicable disease or genetic disease while in the care of the breeder. Some owners will have fallen in love with the puppy quickly and intend to keep the puppy regardless of health problems, but others, particularly those intending to compete with the dog, may prefer to return the puppy to the care of the breeder. The contract should state under what circumstances a full refund is appropriate.

Many breeders also include a clause stating that they are willing to take the dog back at any time with no questions asked. This is intended to ensure the safety and well-being of the dog throughout its lifetime. Many breeders would prefer to find a new home for the dog themselves, rather than risk the dog going to a shelter where it may be euthanized or sent to an inappropriate home.

Photo Courtesy of
Debbie Jones

When you receive your contract from the breeder, it's important to read the document thoroughly. Instead of signing the contract immediately, take a few days to read it over and consider whether you have any questions or need to make any changes to the document. If you have any concerns, you need to discuss them with the breeder before signing the contract. Remember, the contract is a legally binding document, so you need to be sure that you understand what you're agreeing to before you commit to signing it.

Choosing the Perfect Puppy

"The most important thing you can do is to pick your puppy after you have spent hours with him/her over several days. The puppy will pick you if you let it, and they know better than you."

James C Beel
ACD Breeder

When faced with a litter of adorable Australian Cattle Dog puppies, choosing just one can seem like a daunting task. However, if you've discussed your needs and goals with your breeder, he or she may be able to help guide you through making this difficult choice. Remember, the breeder has been with the puppies every day since they were born and has observed as their personalities have developed. There is no better person to help you make your choice. If you've thoroughly described your ideal dog to the breeder, you may not need to make a choice if there is only one puppy that meets your needs. At the very least, the breeder will be able to narrow down your choices to just a couple puppies, which can be much less overwhelming than having to choose from an entire litter.

Although it may be difficult, it's important to remember that a puppy's appearance should be the least of your concerns. It can be easy to get caught up on how a puppy looks, especially if you have a color preference. However, if you're looking for an outgoing, gregarious puppy and end up taking home a nervous, shy puppy because it was the right color, you may end up disappointed. The puppy of your dreams may not look exactly as you imagined, but if the temperament and performance potential are right, then you need to base your decision on those qualities rather than just appearance.

Tips for Adopting an Australian Cattle Dog

"When looking for a dog from a rescue - take your time; ask those working directly with the dog about what they have observed when handling the dog. How does the dog socialize with others? Have they tested the dog in different every day scenarios: food aggression, with children, with other dogs or with other types of pets? Cattle dogs can commonly be aloof or reserved in shelters, how do they react to you once they are alone with you in a visiting yard where there is less activity?"

Kelsey Bolton
Flintlock Farms

If you've decided to adopt an Australian Cattle Dog from a shelter or rescue organization rather than buy from a breeder, it's still important to be able to picture your ideal dog. Having a rough idea of what you're looking for will help guide you in your search for the perfect dog. Rather than inquiring about specific dogs, you may want to contact rescue staff or volunteers to discuss your needs. If they don't have a dog that suits you at the moment, they may be able to keep an eye out or put you in touch with another rescue organization.

Before you begin your search, you also need to decide if there are any deal breakers that could ruin a potential adoption. If there are certain behavioral problems you aren't willing to take on, you need to decide on what you are and are not willing to work with before you start looking for a dog. It's not uncommon for shelter dogs to have been given up due to behavioral or training issues, even if many of these bad habits are relatively easy to solve. Some dogs will need more training than others, so you need to decide how much work you're willing to put into training your new dog. Some behaviors, such as aggression or fearfulness, can be difficult to fix and may require serious dedication to a dog's training, while bad habits such as chewing or digging may be easier to solve.

If you have other pets or children at home, you'll need to discuss them with the shelter staff. Some dogs may need to be placed in homes without other pets or they may not like children, so it's important to consider this before bringing the dog home. Transitioning into a new home is stressful enough for a dog and you don't want anyone to be injured or to have to return the dog to the shelter because it didn't get along with other family members. Most shelters will require or at least suggest that you bring your other pets and kids in to meet the dog before allowing you to take it home to prevent such problems.

Many rescue organizations require potential adopters to not only fill out an application form, but to undergo a home check as well. A home check consists of a rescue volunteer coming to your house to make sure it's a safe environment for a dog. Don't worry, they are not there to judge you or pry into your personal life, they simply want to make sure it's the right home for the dog. If there are any potential concerns, the volunteer will likely discuss them with you to find a solution to the problem before you will be able to bring home a dog.

If you aren't entirely ready to commit to the decision to adopt a dog, you may want to consider volunteering as a foster home for a

Photo Courtesy of Natalia Gutierrez

short period of time. You'll probably have to jump through the same hoops as a potential adopter would, but if things don't work out with the dog, you'll be able to send it along to another foster home or adopter. In the meantime, you'll be able to give a dog a loving home until a more permanent solution can be found. Fostering keeps dogs out of stressful shelter environments, keeping them calm, well behaved, and more likely to find a forever home. If you fall in love with the dog you're fostering, you can always apply for adoption to make the arrangement more permanent.

CHAPTER 3
Preparing Your Home for Your New Australian Cattle Dog

Adjusting Your Current Pets and Children

Introducing a new dog into your household can seem like a daunting task, but if your introductions are done properly, you should have little to worry about. Remember, some family members may need more time to adjust to the change, so go slowly and take as much time as necessary. Rushing through introductions can leave pets or children upset or frightened, so it's important that you dedicate the necessary time and effort to introducing them properly.

Setting up a dedicated area for your new Australian Cattle Dog will help ease him into your household by giving him a place that he can call his own. This space should ideally be somewhere that he can see the activity of the house, but can still retreat to the comfort of his own space if needed. This will also give your current pets or children the opportunity to interact with the new dog without causing anyone undue stress.

Photo Courtesy of Mikayla Franklin

If possible, introductions should always be performed on neutral territory. Some pets can become territorial if introduced to a new animal on their own turf, so setting the meeting up on neutral ground will allow them the opportunity to get to know each other without worrying about territory. If you're bringing home an Australian Cattle Dog from a shelter or foster home, you may be able to introduce your pets in a dedicated meeting room or outside space. If you don't have this luxury, try to find a space where your current pets don't spend much time. This could be a local park or even your front yard. Use caution when introducing unvaccinated or undervaccinated puppies in public places. If your puppy hasn't yet received all of his vaccines, you may want to try introducing him to your family in a low-traffic area of your home, such as an office, guest bedroom, or formal dining room. The less time your current pets spend in that area, the less likely they are to become territorial over it.

Some pets may not be as willing to accept a new member of the family as others. It's important to take your time during these difficult introductions. Never push the animals closer together than they are comfortable with. They may react out of fear or aggression. Your goal is for everyone to get along while still respecting their personal space. If your puppy's first introduction to the family doesn't go as planned, don't panic just yet. If you've set up a separate space for your puppy, your current pets can become familiar with the sounds and smells of a new dog, thus relieving some of their anxiety. Try short introductory sessions throughout your puppy's first few days at home. With each session, you may find that your pets are more comfortable being near each other.

Dangerous Things That Dogs Might Eat

Before bringing your Australian Cattle Dog home for the first time, you need to thoroughly puppy-proof your home. Remember, puppies often explore their environment with their mouths, so it's important to make sure there is nothing dangerous that your new dog may be able to eat.

The most obvious dangers in any household are pest control and cleaning products. Make sure all hazardous chemicals are locked away out of reach of your new puppy. Some puppies are nosy enough to figure out how to open cabinet doors, so you may need to consider placing toddler-proof locks on your cabinets. You might also consider placing toxic products on high shelves that your dog won't be able to reach, or in a garage or room that the dog is not allowed into. If you're struggling with a pest problem, rather than treating the problem with harsh chemicals, consider consulting pest control professionals. They may be able to recommend a more pet-friendly solution to your problems.

Another household danger to watch out for is antifreeze. If your new puppy will have access to any place frequented by vehicles, you need to make sure that the vehicles present do not have any antifreeze leaks. Antifreeze has a sweet taste that is appealing to animals, so if they find it, they are likely to lick up as much as they can. Ethylene glycol is the toxic compound in antifreeze and if ingested it can cause vomiting, drunken or wobbly movements, rapid heart rate, seizures, and even coma or death. If you find a leak in your vehicle, it's im-

Photo Courtesy of
Samantha Runyon

portant to get it repaired as quickly as possible. Even if your dog doesn't have access to the area, other neighborhood pets and animals are still at risk.

If you have children in your home, you'll need to keep a close eye on their toys. Encourage them to pick up their toys after they're done playing so that the puppy won't have the oppor-

FUN FACT
Coat Colors

Australian Cattle Dogs come in two colors: red merle and blue merle. These coats are typically speckled (light spots on a dark background) but they can be mottled (dark spots on a light background).

tunity to chew on or accidentally ingest them. Small toys or pieces of toys can cause intestinal blockages, which can be fatal if left untreated. Surgery is the only option for removing intestinal blockages and it can be expensive and require significant recovery time. Additionally, some children may become upset or resentful toward the puppy after having a favorite toy destroyed. Keeping toys in containers or on shelves can help discourage your puppy from chewing on any of your children's toys.

Whether you have just a few houseplants or you live in a miniature jungle, you need to make sure that all of your houseplants are safe to have around dogs. A simple internet search can reveal whether a plant is toxic to dogs. Common houseplants such as calla lilies, birds of paradise, and eucalyptus can be toxic if ingested. If you have toxic plants that you can't live without, be sure to place them somewhere that your puppy will never be able to reach. In fact, even if your houseplants are not toxic, it's a good idea to keep them away from your puppy. It can be frustrating to come home after a long day of work to find broken pots, soil, and chewed up plants strewn around your home.

An often overlooked source of danger is your trash can. Trash cans are often tempting to curious puppies because of the interesting smells and leftover food. Depending on your family, your trash may contain human food that is toxic to dogs, cleaning products, broken items, or disposable plastics. If your puppy gets into the trash, he is at risk of poisoning and potential intestinal blockages or punctures. Once a puppy discovers the wonderful buffet of the trash can, he may be more inclined to seek it out, so you need to be sure that you keep your trash in a secure location. Ideally, your trash can be kept inside a cabinet or closet that remains closed or locked. There are also a variety of trash cans on the market designed to discourage pets from getting into them. Some are able to be locked shut and others are heavy enough not to be knocked over. Your solution to the problem will depend on the layout of your house and how interested in trash your puppy is.

Other Household Dangers

If your home has a pool, you need to ensure that your puppy can't gain unsupervised access to the pool area. If the pool is surrounded by a fence, it's important to walk the perimeter of the fence to make sure there are no areas where your Australian Cattle Dog could squeeze between or under the rails. If the spaces between the rails are large enough for a puppy to fit through, you may want to consider lining the bottom half the fence with wire mesh, such as the type of fencing used for chickens or gardening. If your pool doesn't have a fence, for the safety of your pets and family, you may want to consider having one installed. If a new fence is not possible, you must be certain that your dog can't access the pool area unless he is under strict supervision. Even the best doggy swimmers can panic when they find themselves in a pool and they may not be able to find the stairs in time.

Power cords also pose a danger to inquisitive puppies. While exploring his new home, your puppy may mistake an electrical cord for an interesting new toy, so make sure that there are no cords within his reach.

Photo Courtesy of
Mandie Gallier

Preparing an Inside Space for Your Australian Cattle Dog

"It is best to be prepared for a feisty puppy! You should at minimum have a size appropriate crate, foldable exercise pen, food and water dishes, chew proof toys, treats for training, proper dog food as discussed with your vet, puppy pads and patience! Do not allow your puppy to be unsupervised in your home until they have had time to adjust and grow, control the situation to avoid trouble early on. Have a safe place for your puppy to rest, and to not disturb you over night when most puppies are the most difficult."

Kelsey Bolton
Flintlock Farms

Before you bring your Australian Cattle Dog home for the first time, you need to dedicate a space in your home for your new dog to stay for the first few weeks or months. Smaller spaces or those with easy-to-clean floors such as laundry rooms, bathrooms, or even a section of the kitchen often work well. Dogs generally prefer not to relieve themselves near their eating or sleeping areas, so smaller spaces are best for puppies or adults who are not yet housetrained. While your new dog is adjusting to life in a new home, it can be helpful to have his space near a heavily trafficked area of your home if possible. This way he won't feel isolated and can get used to your family without being underfoot.

The first step in setting up your dog's space is to get down on his eye level to make sure there are no hidden dangers in the room that you might otherwise miss. Puppy-proofing is essential to the safety of your new family member, so be sure to thoroughly check the area and remove any potential dangers that he could eat, chew on, or get into. You'll also need to make sure the area is secure. If you're using a playpen or pressure-mounted baby gate, make sure that your puppy can't squeeze through the bars or otherwise escape.

Once the area has been deemed safe, you can begin setting up your puppy's supplies. It can be helpful to line the floor with disposable puppy pads. As long as your puppy doesn't chew on them, these pads can be a convenient way to clean up inevitable messes. If you notice your Australian

Cattle Dog chewing on the puppy pads, you may need to remove them as they can potentially be ingested and cause an intestinal blockage.

If your puppy's space has an obvious entrance, such as a gate or door-way, you'll want to avoid placing his food and water dishes in this area. He may become excited when he realizes it's time for a walk or when you come home after work and can easily knock over his food or water. Instead, consider placing his bedding near the entrance. This way, your puppy can rest comfortably while waiting for you to return.

Preparing Outside Spaces

Outdoor puppy-proofing should be done in the same manner as your home. It may seem silly to wander around your yard on your hands and knees, but it can be incredibly helpful in finding potential dangers to your new puppy. Take your time and be sure to check every corner of your outside space to ensure there is nothing that could potentially harm your new family member.

Photo Courtesy of Brianna Camp

If your property is fenced, you'll need to walk along every inch of the fence line to check for possible escape routes. Gaps between boards, holes under the fence, or even loose boards could allow your puppy to leave the yard without your knowledge. The world outside your property is dangerous for an unaccompanied puppy, so you want to make sure there is no way he can escape your yard.

If your yard has any off-limits areas, make sure they are secure. Pools, garden areas, and garages are often quite dangerous for curious puppies, so it's best if these areas are fenced off and all gates and doors are shut. If you have a basement, make sure that there is no way your puppy could fall into the window wells. Your local home improvement store likely has quite a few options to cover your window wells without being a fire hazard.

Whether you have a vegetable garden, flower bed, or professional landscaping, it's important to make sure that your yard doesn't contain any poisonous plants. Your puppy will likely take a nibble of the plants in your outdoor space at some point, so be sure there is nothing that could harm him. If you do have toxic plants, or you simply would prefer that your puppy didn't destroy your garden, consider making certain areas off-limits by setting up a small fence or barrier. Not only will a barrier help keep your puppy safe from toxic plants, but it well help keep your beautiful flowers or vegetables safe.

Supplies

If you have other dogs in your home, you probably won't need to purchase too many supplies for your new puppy. However, even if you have most of the items you'll need, you should still make a complete list to be sure you aren't missing anything. Bringing home a new puppy is stressful anyway, so you want to avoid that last-minute panic when you realize you forgot to buy puppy food. If your current pets are territorial or would prefer not to share their favorite toys or beds, you may want to consider purchasing a few new items for your puppy. Bedding that doesn't smell like strange dogs will also help your new dog settle into your home more quickly.

If you're bringing home an Australian Cattle Dog puppy, or an adult who hasn't yet been housetrained, you'll need to pick up a few supplies to help with housetraining. Disposable puppy pads, as mentioned before, are a great way to help keep your new dog's space clean. If you work long hours, your puppy may not be able to hold it until you get home, so training your puppy to use absorbent pads in your absence can be helpful until he's old enough to hold it through the workday. Your local pet store or favorite online retailer likely has a selection of cleaning supplies made specifically for pet messes. Most of these cleaners contain enzymes to eliminate odor and discourage any future messes in that area. You may also want to consider bells for your door to help your puppy learn how to get your attention when he needs to go out. Australian Cattle Dogs are incredibly intelligent and learn quickly that nudging or pawing at bells will get you to take them outside.

Regardless of what type of food you intend to feed your new dog, you'll need to find out what type of food the breeder or shelter was feeding him. Suddenly switching foods can cause digestive upset, so buy a small amount of the old food and slowly mix it with the new food. During your puppy's first week at home, you can begin introducing small amounts of the new food with each meal, increasing it until he's eating only the new food. Check with your breeder or shelter staff as they may be able to provide you with a small amount of the old food to use during this transition.

It can be stressful for a puppy to leave his mother and littermates for a new home, so provide as much comfort as possible. Although your puppy will eventually love his cozy new bed with blankets to burrow in, the strange smells of your home and your other pets may put your puppy on edge for the first few days. If your breeder does not provide one, ask if you can leave

Photo Courtesy of
Nicole Bonner

a blanket with your puppy and his littermates for a few days before you take him home. The blanket can absorb the familiar smells of the breeder's home, providing your puppy with a sense of comfort during the stressful transition into your family.

Don't forget to provide your puppy with an appropriately sized collar and leash. Most types of collars are adjustable so they can grow with your puppy. You may need to estimate the correct size, but many collar manufacturers provide a sizing guide on their packaging. Remember to pick up an identification tag or plate for your puppy's collar as well. Even if you've properly puppy-proofed your home and yard, your puppy may still find a way to get lost so it's best to make sure he can be properly identified if found by your neighbors.

Australian Cattle Dogs are relatively low-maintenance when it comes to grooming, but you may still want to have a few grooming supplies on hand. A brush designed for short-haired dogs, such as a rubber curry brush or bristle brush, can help get your dog used to the grooming process and help keep him from shedding all over your house. You may also want to pick up a shampoo or waterless shampoo wipes to help keep your puppy clean. If you intend to do all your dog's grooming rather than take him to a professional, you'll also need to pick up a nail trimmer or grinder. If you aren't sure what products are best for Australian Cattle Dogs, try asking a professional groomer. Groomers are experts in helping dogs to look and feel great, so they're a great source of information for at-home coat care.

CHAPTER 4

Bringing Home Your New Australian Cattle Dog

"These dogs are highly active, and want to be with their owners as much as possible. They require a solid and ongoing foundation of obedience training and socialization. While they are wonderful livestock working dogs, they can also be successful at many other activities that require a dog to be physically and mentally active, such as rally, obedience, disc or fly ball, barn hunting, search and rescue or a hiking/running buddy."

Gwen Shepperson
Buffalo Creek Cattle Dogs

The Importance of Having a Plan

Photo Courtesy of Tiffany Hughes

Thoroughly planning the arrival of your new Australian Cattle Dog does not mean you won't run into problems, but it can help you react to those problems appropriately with as little stress as possible for both you and your dog. For some owners, writing their plan out on a piece of paper gives them peace of mind as they have a physical resource to look to if something goes awry. Regardless of how you develop your plan, the most important aspect is that you're as prepared as you can be. Planning your puppy's arrival and consulting a list through each step of the process can help prevent panic when you run into problems.

Photo Courtesy of
Shantele Rogers

The Ride Home

When you pick up your Australian Cattle Dog from the breeder or shelter, it's important to consider that this may be the dog's first time in a car. Unless you know for a fact that your new dog is an experienced traveler, you need to prepare as if it's his first time. You want to make this car ride a good experience for him so that he'll be more willing to travel with you in the future, even if it's only an occasional trip to the vet. No matter how your dog reacts to the car, you need to stay as calm as possible. Your puppy will sense your anxiety, but he may not understand that you're responding to his behavior rather than the car. This can cause him to become more anxious or panic.

The most important aspect of your dog's ride home is restraint. An unrestrained dog in the car presents a danger not only to you but to other drivers as well. There are several different options to consider when it comes to restraining your dog. For young puppies or adults with an unknown history, a crate kennel is often the best option. Wire or plastic kennels come in a variety of sizes to fit most vehicles. The kennel will keep your dog secure, even if he is a nervous traveler. Some dogs find comfort in having their kennels covered in the car while others prefer to see out the window, so use your best judgment on which your dog would prefer. An additional benefit of using a kennel is how easy they are to clean, should your dog become carsick. As your dog gains more experience riding in the car, you may want to try out oth-

Photo Courtesy of
Tiffany Hughes

er methods of restraint, such as doggy seat belts or barriers, but for the first trip, a crate or kennel should suffice.

FUN FACT
Born White

All Australian Cattle Dog puppies are born white. They gain their red or blue color as they grow and usually have their adult color by six weeks of age.

Even dogs who have traveled extensively can become carsick on occasion, so it can be helpful to be prepared. Waterproof seat covers are a great way to protect your car's interior, but blankets or towels work well too. If your dog is traveling in a crate, you can line the crate with disposable, absorbent puppy pads or washable towels or blankets. Many crates have a removable tray that can simply be hosed off. Remember, even if your puppy gets carsick, you need to stay as calm as possible. You may also want to consider bringing along a blanket from the breeder or shelter to provide the dog with a soothing and familiar smell.

The First Night Home

"The first few weeks are definitely the hardest! Be prepared for a busy puppy if you buy a young ACD. Set a high standard from day one and a set schedule; do not tolerate chewing, yipping or chasing. If you are bringing home an adult dog, be prepared to mentally exercise your dog as well as physically. They will be looking to establish dominance or pecking order in their new home, including the animals already established in the home. Do not let the first few weeks deter you; it is a transition period that should be given the utmost patience to establish a routine and acceptable behaviors."

Kelsey Bolton
Flintlock Farms

If possible, you should plan to bring your new Australian Cattle Dog home the night before you have a day off. It's unlikely that you're going to have a particularly restful night. The first night in a new home can be stressful for a dog of any age, but this is especially true for puppies. This may be your puppy's first night away from the familiar surroundings of the breeder's home, so he may be upset. Some adult dogs may also be distressed by the change, so it's essential that you try to make the night as relaxing as possible. If you've prepared your home and have the necessary supplies, you should be ready for your new dog's first night home.

Before bringing your dog home, you need to consider where he'll spend his first night. If you've set up an area for him in a more heavily trafficked area of your home, decide whether he will sleep there or in a crate or play-pen in your bedroom. It can be tempting to put him as far away as possible if he begins crying or howling, but isolation may only make him more upset. It's not advisable to have a new dog sleep in your bed. Until you know your Australian Cattle Dog is fully housetrained, it's best to let him sleep in either a crate or playpen.

To encourage your puppy to rest peacefully, you should try to keep him calm in the hours leading up to bedtime. This is not a time for roughhousing or vigorous walks. You want him to learn that bedtime is a time to relax and be calm, so try to exercise or play with him earlier in the day. Vigorous play sessions earlier in the day will also help him calm down later in the evening.

Photo Courtesy of
Cassy Moore

If possible, try to keep the same bedtime schedule every day. This will help your puppy understand what is expected of him. No matter what your bedtime schedule is like, you should make your puppy's bathroom break the last task before heading to bed. With young puppies or adults who haven't been housetrained, you'll still need to go out every few hours during the night, but taking your dog out as late as possible will help you get a little more sleep between trips outside.

Your puppy may become distressed once you've settled into bed and turned out the lights. Remember, your puppy doesn't understand why he's been taken away from his siblings, so he may cry or howl. It can be difficult not to respond to these cries, but if you acknowledge your puppy every time he makes a noise, you are only teaching him that barking or howling will get him attention. Do not yell at him or scold him for this behavior. Instead, try to ignore him. Eventually, he will understand that his noise won't get him attention and he'll settle down. However, you will need to learn the differences between cries for attention and cries to go outside. If it's been a few hours since your puppy's last trip outside, you may want to take him out just to be sure.

First Vet Visit/Choosing a Vet

The best way to find a reputable veterinarian is through recommendations. If you have friends or family who own dogs, ask them where they take their dogs for veterinary care. Your breeder may also be able to recommend a good vet. A quick internet search will also show you what veterinary clinics are available in your area. Many search engines or websites allow users to post reviews of local businesses, so you may be able to read the reviews of local clinics and make your decision accordingly.

During your puppy's first vet visit, the veterinarian will likely perform a brief physical examination to make sure he's in good health. Your puppy will be also be weighed so that the vet can establish a baseline by which to monitor his weight as he grows. The vet will listen to your new dog's heart and lungs and examine his teeth, eyes, and ears. You may also be asked about your dog's eating and drinking habits, as well as his diet. If you have any concerns about your Australian Cattle Dog's health, now is the time to ask.

Your puppy may be due for vaccines during his first trip to the vet, so it's important that you bring along any medical information from the breeder or shelter. The vet can look over the information and make sure your puppy is up to date on all vaccines. Along with vaccines, your dog may be checked

Photo Courtesy of
Matilda Kitcker

for parasites and dewormed. Intestinal worms are common in puppies, so even if your dog isn't showing signs of worms, your vet may opt to administer a dewormer anyway.

During your first visit, your vet may want to discuss microchipping your puppy. Microchipping is a simple procedure in which a small microchip is inserted beneath your dog's skin, just above his withers. The microchip is similar in size to a grain of rice and can be detected by any approved scanner. If your dog becomes lost, regardless of whether he has a collar on, a microchip means he can be identified by any shelter or veterinary clinic. Microchipping is not required, but it is highly recommended.

If you've adopted your Australian Cattle Dog from a shelter, your new dog may already be spayed or neutered. If not, most vets recommended altering at around six months of age, so even if your puppy isn't quite old enough, it's a good idea to start discussing any concerns you may have with your vet. You may also be able to get an estimated cost for the procedure, so you can start budgeting if necessary. Remember that there may be stipulations in the breeder contract about spaying or neutering.

Puppy Classes

Teaching your puppy basic obedience is often easier when you have a little help. You may want to consider finding local puppy classes. In addition to basic socialization, your puppy will learn how to walk on a leash without pulling, come when called, and a few other simple commands. Puppy classes are also a great place to seek advice on housetraining and bad habit prevention.

Some classes may require puppies to be a certain age or have certain vaccinations before they are allowed to attend. Check with the trainer or facility offering the classes to make sure your puppy will be allowed to participate. Adult dogs are not usually allowed in puppy classes, but the same trainer or facility may offer other basic obedience classes, so be sure to research your options.

Depending on where you live, you may have quite a few options for puppy classes. If you've adopted your dog from a shelter, you may want to ask shelter staff about upcoming obedience classes, as they often offer such classes as fundraisers for the facility. You may also be able to find formal obedience schools or individual trainers offering their services. It's a good idea to check out a few different options before committing to make sure you're signing up for a quality class. If your puppy isn't old enough, or your dog has a few behavior problems, you may want to consider consulting a private trainer that can help you in your home before taking your dog to a group session.

Cost Breakdown for the First Year

The first year of dog ownership can be quite costly, so it's important to consider whether you are ready to take on the financial responsibility of a dog. If you're living paycheck to paycheck you may need to reconsider getting a dog. However, if you are truly committed to bringing a dog into your home, it may be manageable with proper budgeting.

If you plan on adopting an Australian Cattle Dog from a shelter, the first expense you'll encounter is the adoption fee. Depending on the shelter or rescue organization, this can range up to a few hundred dollars. Dogs adopted from shelters generally have been spayed or neutered and are up to date on all vaccines, so you'll save some money on veterinary care.

If you choose to purchase a dog from a reputable breeder, your initial expense will be much bigger. Purebred puppies can cost anywhere from $700 to a few thousand dollars. The price is typically based on the breeder's health testing and the performance records of their dogs. You will also need to budget for your puppy's initial veterinary care such as vaccinations, deworming, and spaying or neutering. Although the purchase price is more than you would pay for a rescue, you'll likely be getting a dog with some type of health guarantee.

The initial cost of your new Australian Cattle Dog is not the only expense you need to consider. Supplies and routine veterinary care can add up quickly. Depending on the area in which you live and your choice in food and supplies, you may be spending anywhere from $1,000 to over $3,400 during your first year of dog ownership. Here is a breakdown of the potential costs you may encounter during your first year:

Mandatory Expenses	Cost Estimate
Food	$300 - $900
Food and Water Dishes	$10 - $50
Treats	$50 - $150
Toys	$20 - $200
Collars and Leashes	$10 - $100
Crate	$25 - $100
Dog Beds	$25 - $100
Vaccines and Routine Veterinary Care	$100 - $350
Heartworm Testing	$10 - $35
Heartworm Prevention	$25 - $125
Flea and Tick Prevention	$40 - $200
Spaying or Neutering	$150 - $600
Puppy Classes	$200 - $500
Total	$965 - $3,410

Unfortunately, supplies, training, and routine veterinary care are not the only expenses you'll need to budget for. If you are not able or willing to groom your dog yourself, you'll need to consider the cost of professional grooming. Though Australian Cattle Dogs are a relatively low-maintenance breed, you'll still likely spend somewhere between $30 and $60 per grooming session. Most groomers recommend appointments every six to eight weeks, so you'll need to make sure you can afford this cost. Many owners are happy to have professionals deal with the hassle of grooming, but if money is tight you may need to do this yourself.

The biggest potential cost, and the most difficult to budget for, is emergency veterinary care. Unfortunately, accidents can and will happen and they can be quite costly. Emergency or after-hours veterinary care can range from just a few hundred dollars to several thousand. Many owners choose to set aside a small amount each month to help budget for emergency care if the need arises.

If you plan on traveling without your dog, you'll also need to consider the cost of pet sitting or boarding. Depending on your area and the services offered by the sitter or boarding facility, you may be paying over $100 per day. Of course, if you bring your dog with you or have friends or family who can care for your pets while you're away, you may be able to avoid this expense.

Possible Expenses	Cost Estimate
Professional Grooming	$100 - $500
Emergency Veterinary Services	$200 - $1,000+
Pet Sitting or Boarding	$15 - $100+ per day

The expenses in this section may seem overwhelming but they are not meant to deter you from bringing home an Australian Cattle Dog. Being prepared for the potential costs of dog ownership will help you to be able to afford your dog's care when extra costs arise. Bringing a dog into your household is a big responsibility and you need to carefully consider whether you are prepared to spend the money necessary for proper care. Careful consideration and planning are the best options for providing for your dog without putting unnecessary strain on your financial situation.

Photo Courtesy of
Mandie Gallier

CHAPTER 5
Being a Puppy Parent

"This breed will require a take charge attitude, or your cattle dog will quickly take that role for you. They have been bred for over a century to be a tough, thick headed go getter, tough enough to push wild stock through some of the most rugged terrain in the outback. They are not a meek breed. They are looking for a handler to be in charge and to give them a job, even if that job is not pushing cattle across the back country. You must know you are in control of your dog, or you will find behavioral issues are common for this highly intelligent breed."

Kelsey Bolton
Flintlock Farms

Standing by Your Expectations

Raising an Australian Cattle Dog puppy is a full-time job, so it's important to be realistic about your expectations of both yourself and your puppy. Between exercise, training, and supervision, puppies require a lot of commitment, so you need to make sure that you are able to devote enough time to your new dog. The more time you are able to spend working with your puppy, the more quickly he'll learn the rules of the house and progress in his training. If you're only able to hold one or two training sessions a week, your puppy won't learn as fast as if you hold one or more five-minute training sessions each day.

For the first few weeks after bringing your Australian Cattle Dog home, you need to have particularly low expectations for your puppy. Remember, this is a new situation for you both, but your puppy's world is much smaller than your own and change can be scary. Of course, it's important to begin training as soon as possible, but you need to be patient as your puppy adapts to his new life and everyone gets to know each other. Expecting too much from your puppy too soon can lead to disappointment and frustration.

Photo Courtesy of
Isabelle Dirks

How to Crate Train

"If you are planning to crate train make sure you are consistent. If the pup is whining or carrying on loudly DO NOT let it out of the crate until it calms down. This will translate later into a dog that is quiet and calm in his/her crate."

Kacy VanDuinen
Triple M Corgis (and Cattle Dogs)

Crate training is an essential skill that your dog will need throughout his lifetime. Eventually, you may need to leave your dog in the care of a groomer or veterinary team, and they may need to keep him in a crate until they are ready to work on him. Dogs who haven't been properly crate trained may bark or relieve themselves due to stress. As you may imagine, these behaviors will not make your dog a welcome guest at any facility. It's also common for dogs who haven't been crate trained to dig or chew at the crate doors or walls, potentially damaging their teeth or nails in the process. To prevent unnecessary injuries and to reduce stress on both your dog and anyone who will work with him in the future, crate training is highly recommended.

In order to successfully crate train your new Australian Cattle Dog, make sure his crate is an appealing place to spend time. Placing the crate in a quiet corner, out of the way but with a good view of the action, will give your dog a comfortable place to rest while still allowing him to keep an eye on his new family. If you're certain that your puppy won't chew on his bedding, you can try placing his favorite bed or blanket inside the crate to provide him with warmth and comfort. While you're at home, it's a good idea to keep the crate door open to give your dog access to his crate whenever he wants. The more comfortable you make the crate, the more likely he is to spend time there of his own accord.

Initially, your dog may be hesitant about spending long periods of time in his crate. Rather than shoving him inside, try to entice him to enter on his own by tossing a few treats inside. He may grab the treats and back out immediately, but with practice he'll become more comfortable in the crate. Eventually, you can begin shutting the door behind him. Encourage him to wait patiently in the crate for a few seconds before opening the door. As he progresses in his training, you can leave him in the crate for short periods of time while you're still present. This can be a good opportunity to get a few household chores done without a curious puppy underfoot. If your dog begins to bark or cry while in the crate, it's essential that you wait until he's calmed down before releasing him. If you release him while he's making noise, you're only rewarding his bad behavior. With practice and plenty of praise, your dog will learn that the crate is a comfortable place to spend his time and that there's no reason to fret.

Photo Courtesy of
Regan Miller

Chewing

"They are going to chew, period. They have to. They are teething. Get them something to chew and put away everything you do not want to be chewed."

James C Beel
ACD Breeder

Unfortunately, chewing is an inevitable stage of every puppy's life. Between the ages of four and six months, your puppy will begin to lose his baby teeth as his adult teeth come in. This process can be quite painful, so many puppies resort to chewing to relieve some of the discomfort. They may chew shoes, furniture, bedding, and children's toys. Keeping dangerous items, such as electrical cords, out of reach is especially important during this time.

While smaller items, such as shoes or toys, can be picked up and kept out of your puppy's reach, larger items like furniture are harder to remove. Chew-deterrent sprays are a great way to discourage puppies from chewing on furniture, walls, or cabinets. Your local pet store or favorite online retailer likely has a few different options, but most sprays are either bitter apple or spicy pepper flavored. The unpleasant flavor typically discourages chewing rather quickly, but the spray must be reapplied until your puppy is out of the teething stage and learns to leave the object alone.

To further discourage your puppy from chewing on inappropriate objects, you may want to provide him with other, more appropriate options. There is a huge variety of toys on the market designed specifically for chewing. Some toys can even be frozen to provide a cooling sensation to help relieve the discomfort of teething. No matter which type of toy you choose, remember to keep an eye on your puppy during playtime to make sure he hasn't chewed off any chunks. If the toy breaks or is chewed down to a size that might be swallowed, it's time to take the toy away and find a replacement.

HELPFUL TIP
Bite Nipping in the Bud

With any puppy, it's important to teach bite inhibition. It's even more important with Australian Cattle Dogs because they were bred to nip at the heels of cattle. Without consistent bite- inhibition training, they can turn those nipping instincts on humans, especially when "herding" children.

Photo Courtesy of
Kelsey George

Growling and Barking

It's not uncommon for Australian Cattle Dogs to be standoffish or aloof around strangers, but aggressive or fearful behavior, such as growling or barking, should be discouraged. It might be cute to see a puppy acting so tough, but if this aggression is left uncorrected it can escalate into a more serious problem.

If your puppy begins to growl or bark at people or other pets, distraction may be your best tool. Clap your hands loudly, stomp your foot, or firmly tell him "No." Never try to comfort your puppy when he is behaving in a fearful or aggressive manner. Babying or coddling him will only encourage him to act this way in the future. Once the growling or barking has stopped, praise your puppy or reward him with treats. As you progress with socializing your dog, it's likely that these corrections will become more infrequent.

Digging

Digging is a dangerous habit that should be discouraged. In addition to the possibility of digging under the fence and escaping the yard, dogs who dig can severely damage their nails and paws. They may also ingest sticks, dirt, or rocks. Even if your dog doesn't injure himself while digging, having to constantly fill in holes in your yard or garden can be frustrating.

Digging can only be prevented or corrected with constant supervision. If you allow your dog unsupervised access to your yard or garden, you are giving him the chance to dig without consequences. Inconsistent corrections will not solve the problem, so you must be willing to go with your dog every time he goes outside. When you see him begin to dig, you need to interrupt this behavior with a loud clap or a sharp "No." If you're consistent in your corrections, he will eventually lose interest in digging and wander off to find something else to do.

Separation Anxiety

One of the most frustrating dog habits to deal with is separation anxiety. It can be incredibly difficult to correct, so it's best to prevent the behavior from developing in the first place. Symptoms of separation anxiety can include pacing, panting, drooling, and excessive barking. Some dogs may also become destructive, chewing up your furniture or relieving themselves

Photo Courtesy of Megan Stanton

in the house. Attempts to confine dogs with separation anxiety can result in the dogs becoming injured in an attempt to escape. If your Australian Cattle Dog has developed separation anxiety, consult a professional dog trainer as soon as possible.

From the moment you bring your Australian Cattle Dog home, it's important that you don't make a big deal out of leaving the house or coming home. Drawn out goodbyes and excited hellos only serve to stress your dog out. The less concerned you seem when leaving or arriving, the more your dog will understand that there's no need to worry. Although it can be hard to walk out the door without saying goodbye, just know that you're doing what's best for your dog. Similarly, when you get home, it's essential that you wait until your dog calms down before acknowledging him. Take your time putting your things away and when your dog has settled down then calmly greet him.

If your Australian Cattle Dog is an only pet, you may want to consider getting him a companion to help prevent loneliness in your absence. As pack animals, dogs often behave better when they have another animal to keep them company. A companion can be especially important if you work long hours. Remember, you may have a life outside of your dog, but your dog is incapable of having a life outside of you.

If you've gone through the effort of properly crate training your dog, a crate can be helpful in preventing or correcting separation anxiety because many dogs find comfort in small, cozy spaces. Confinement will also help keep destructive dogs from making a mess of your home. However, if your dog has not been crate trained, crating may only cause him more stress, so only leave your dog in a crate if you trust that he won't try to escape or injure himself.

Running Away

One of the most dangerous habits that a dog can develop is running away. Australian Cattle Dogs are quick, athletic dogs, enabling them to easily stay out of your reach. If your dog bolts out a front door, he may be at risk of running into the street or encountering neighborhood strays or wild animals. Even if your puppy only evades you in your house, he's still behaving badly, and the behavior should be corrected. If you're struggling with your puppy constantly running away, consider consulting a professional trainer before your dog gets hurt.

In the home, you can try what's referred to as a drag lead. Simply attach a short leash to your dog's collar and let him drag it around the house as he goes about his daily activities. The leash is unlikely to bother him, but it will give you a chance to grab or step on it if he tries to sprint out the door or run away from you.

A solid recall is the most important skill for any dog to learn. Your dog needs to learn to come when you call, no matter where he is or what is happening around him. Start teaching this command somewhere quiet and familiar, with few distractions. As your puppy progresses in his training, you can practice recall in your yard, and eventually around your neighborhood and in other public places. The more you practice in different environments, the more likely your dog is to listen when you need him to.

Photo Courtesy of Heather Santella

Photo Courtesy of
Natalia Gutierrez

Bedtime

One of the most important aspects of a good bedtime routine is limiting excitement and physical activity before bed. Bedtime is not the time for a vigorous walk around the neighborhood or an exciting game of fetch. If possible, try to accomplish these activities earlier in the day to help tire your pup out. Providing your dog with plenty of physical and mental stimulation during the day will also encourage calm behavior in the evening hours.

Be sure to take your Australian Cattle Dog outside for his last bathroom break just before bedtime. This is especially important if you are still working on housetraining. With young puppies, you'll still need to get up every few hours, but if you can take your puppy out just before going to bed you may be able to get a few hours of sleep before the next trip out. Try to stick to the same routine every night to help your dog understand what is expected of him.

Leaving Your Australian Cattle Dog Home Alone

During the first few weeks with your Australian Cattle Dog, you may find it distressing to leave him home alone. Thorough preparation is key in developing good manners and preventing separation anxiety. Make sure your puppy is secure in his designated area and that you've removed any potentially dangerous items from the space. Even if you've already puppy-proofed his personal space, it doesn't hurt to take one more look around.

To limit the stress on both you and your dog, you may want to first practice leaving for short periods of time while you're at home. Place your puppy in his designated area for a few minutes while you take out the trash or get the mail. Your puppy will eventually learn that you'll be back soon, and your departure is nothing to worry about. Once he gets used to being left alone for a few moments, you can begin increasing the amount of time that you leave him for.

As previously mentioned, it's essential that you do not make a big deal out of your arrival or departure. Staying calm and not acknowledging your dog's excitement is key to preventing separation anxiety. If you start practicing calm entrances and exits as soon as you bring your puppy home, your puppy will grow up to be a well-adjusted adult who doesn't mind being left alone for a few hours. With enough practice, you'll be able to go to work or run errands knowing that your Australian Cattle Dog is resting quietly at home.

CHAPTER 6
Housetraining

"For house-training to be successful, you MUST be consistent with boundaries and the puppy's schedule. Meals should be given at certain predictable times and trips outside to potty should be predetermined."

Alison Whittington
Hardtack Australian Cattle Dogs

Different Options for Housetraining

Before you begin housetraining your new dog, take a few moments to consider the various options you have. Australian Cattle Dogs are incredibly intelligent and are capable of learning the rules of the house quickly. However, they can also learn bad habits fast, so it's essential that you decide on a method of housetraining and remain consistent. Consider your long-term goals for your new dog and keep them in mind while deciding how to housetrain your puppy.

Traditional housetraining is the most popular method of teaching a dog where to relieve himself. With this method, your dog will learn that he is allowed to relieve himself outdoors only and accidents in the house are discouraged. Since most people choose to use this method with their adult dogs, it can be helpful to keep this in mind, even if you choose to complement traditional housetraining with other methods during your dog's first few months at home.

Since young puppies need more frequent bathroom breaks, it's common to use other methods of housetraining until your puppy is old enough to wait until you get home from work. Litter boxes and disposable puppy pads are not commonly used as permanent housetraining solutions for medium- and large-sized dogs, but they are excellent training aids for puppies. If you work long hours or are unable to take your puppy outside as often as he needs, you can encourage your puppy to relieve himself on a disposable puppy pad, washable potty patch, or litter box. By training your dog to use these options, you'll also have fewer messes to clean up after a long day at work.

Photo Courtesy of
Samantha Runyon

The First Few Weeks

Housetraining is not a quick process, but consistency is key during the first few weeks with your new dog. If you aren't consistent, he's likely to become confused. As you get to know your dog, you'll begin to recognize the signs that he needs to go. This may include sniffing, circling, and walking slowly. If your dog starts to act like he needs to relieve himself, take him outside immediately. You should also be prepared to take your puppy outside after all meals and naps. During the first few weeks, you'll probably find yourself taking your dog out every couple hours. As your puppy matures and progresses in his training, you'll be able to take him out less frequently.

The exact age of your puppy will dictate how frequently you should take him outside for a potty break. The general rule of thumb is that your puppy can go for one hour for every month of his age before needing to go out. For example, you should feel comfortable taking a four-month-old puppy out every four hours or so. Of course, you should still keep an eye on your puppy and take him out if he needs to go out sooner, but if you wait much longer than this, you'll likely need to clean up a mess. Unfortunately, this rule also applies at night, so be prepared for a few months of sleepless nights. Eventually, your puppy will be able to hold it through the night and accidents during the day will become less frequent.

Positive Reinforcement

"Routine, routine, routine! Establish a set routine and stick to it! I cannot emphasize enough how important a schedule is for your new dog or puppy, this repetition will be the key to your success in house training your dog. Much in the same way our inclination to wake up at the same time every morning is naturally, if you wake up at that time every single day, your body acclimates to what has become repetitive. Your dog will also acclimate to what has become repetitive on a daily basis. Also if you can take your dog to the same spot every time to potty, this will help establish proper times and places to potty with your dog. Reward your dog for going outside to bolster good behavior, and lastly have patience! Not all dogs learn quickly."

Kelsey Bolton
Flintlock Farms

One of the most popular methods of training is called positive reinforcement. This method works to encourage the dog to repeat a desirable behavior by rewarding him with a positive stimulus whenever he does as required, encouraging the dog to continue to repeat the behavior in the future. The dog eventually learns that he can earn a treat or praise by performing certain tasks. Australian Cattle Dogs are highly intelligent and will learn what is being asked of them with just a few repetitions.

As with all aspects of housetraining, consistency is key. In the beginning, you'll need to consistently reward your puppy for eliminating in the correct location. However, you need to be cautious about the timing of your reward. You want the dog to associate the reward with going to the bathroom, not just with going outside. Your outdoor space may also be a place for playtime, but you need to teach your puppy to focus on relieving himself before he is allowed to play. When you take your puppy outside for a potty break, remain calm and give him your chosen verbal command, such as "go potty." If he tries to play, simply ignore him and repeat your command. As soon as he begins to relieve himself, reward him with verbal praise. It's best to use verbal praise while he's going, as more exciting rewards may distract him. After he's finished, you can give him any tasty treats you have or engage him in an exciting game of tug or chase. If he gets to roam around the yard, only allow him to do so after he's gone to the bathroom.

Photo Courtesy of
Michael and Sheila Palmeter

Photo Courtesy of Kristina Boesoflug

To maximize the positive reinforcement, it's important to use treats that are of high value to your dog. Although some dogs may be content receiving pieces of kibble after a job well done, most dogs are more likely to repeat a desired behavior if they receive something unusual and especially delicious as a reward. Most treats intended for general training are quite small, as they encourage the dog to repeat the behavior but don't allow time to stop and chew or look for crumbs. Using larger or more distracting treats is perfectly fine to use specifically during housetraining. You want your dog to feel as though he's done a good job and since he doesn't need to immediately follow another command it's okay if he takes the time to lick up crumbs or chew on a larger treat. However, you want to be cautious about giving him too large of a reward as you will need him to be hungry enough to repeat the process in a few hours.

If you would prefer to use praise instead of food, again, you need to make the most out of your reward. Simply telling your dog "good boy" probably won't be enough to encourage him to repeat his good behavior. Instead, you want your praise to be over the top. When he relieves himself in the correct place, it's okay to get excited and show him how proud you are. Be enthusiastic, rub his ears, or play with him. In the beginning, you want your puppy to look forward to his reward, so don't be afraid to go a little crazy with your praise.

Crate Training

Most dogs prefer not to mess in the same space in which they sleep, so crates can make a world of difference when housetraining your Australian Cattle Dog. An appropriately sized crate will help discourage your dog from relieving himself indoors while you're away from the house or unable to supervise him. Additionally, crate training has many long-term benefits as well as giving your puppy a safe, comfortable place to go when he feels overwhelmed.

When crate training your puppy, it's important to view the crate as an aid in your training, rather than a place to keep your dog while you're at work. Teaching your dog proper crate manners is a time-consuming process that must be started while you're home and able to supervise. If you only use the crate when you leave the house, your dog may begin to view his time in the crate as a punishment. Not only will this make housetraining more difficult, but your dog may begin to develop separation anxiety. To encourage your dog to relax in the crate, try placing him inside for short periods of time while you do household chores or clean up. If your puppy is able to see you while you work, he'll feel more relaxed about being in the crate. Be sure to praise him when he's being quiet, and you can even drop an occasional treat into the treat if you like. If he barks or cries, simply ignore him until he quiets down again. With practice, you can begin leaving the room for short periods of time to prepare your puppy for being left alone. Remember, the best time to work on crate training is after a potty break and play session. This way, your puppy will be tired out and more likely to relax during his time in the crate.

Crate training can only be successful if the crate you use is appropriately sized for your dog. The crate needs to be large enough for the dog to stand up and turn around comfort-

Photo Courtesy of Julie Timm

Photo Courtesy of
Ashlyn Talley

ably, but not so large as to encourage him to use a section of the crate to relieve himself. If you've brought home a puppy, this may mean that you need to buy a new crate as your dog grows. Some wire crates come with removable panels that can be moved to adjust the crate size for growing puppies. If you choose this type of crate, try to estimate how large your Australian Cattle Dog will be as an adult and pick the size most appropriate for that size dog.

The type of crate you choose should not have any impact on housetraining, it's simply personal preference. Crates can be made out of nearly any material including metal, wire mesh,

HELPFUL TIP
Crate Training

Many people don't like the idea of keeping their dog in a crate. However, you should still train your dog to accept a crate when she is a puppy. Yes, it helps with house-training, but that's not all.

Your Cattle Dog is likely to encounter a kennel at some point in her life. It may be at a groomer, the vet, or doggy day care. If she hasn't already gotten used to being in a kennel, this will be an extremely stressful situation for her. She could even injure herself trying to escape.

Once your dog is used to a crate, you don't need to always close the door. Leave it open and let your dog treat the crate as a safe space.

wood, and plastic. You may find that your dog prefers to have his crate enclosed or covered, in which case you can choose either a more closed off crate, such as the type of plastic crate used for airline travel, or you can buy a fabric cover. If your dog would prefer to see what's happening around him, choose a more open crate style. If you have budget restrictions, this may also dictate the type of crate you buy. Wire and plastic crates tend to be cheaper than those made of wood or metal.

Playpens and Doggy Doors

As your Australian Cattle Dog progresses in his housetraining, you may want to offer him a bit more freedom than the crate while you're away. Playpens and doggy doors allow your dog access to much more space than his crate, so you need to be sure that he can be trusted with his freedom. A playpen can be used as an intermediate step in housetraining, offering your dog more freedom, but not so much that he may find himself getting into trouble. Doggy doors are best left to dogs who can be trusted not to chew or eat inappropriate objects.

Playpens can be made from a variety of materials, including wood, plastic, and wire mesh. They are also available in various heights and diameters. The type of playpen you choose will depend on the age and size of your dog, as well as your own preferences. During housetraining, you may want to line the floor of the pen with disposable puppy pads to help with cleanup should your puppy have an accident. It should be noted that some larger puppies or adult dogs may be able to push over or jump out of a playpen. If you choose a playpen as the next step in housetraining, be sure to let your dog explore the pen in your presence to ensure he can't find his way out.

Doggy doors can be particularly useful when housetraining adult dogs, or puppies that are out of the chewing stage. Doggy doors come in a wide range of sizes and materials. You can find temporary doors that fit in sliding patio doors, or you can find more permanent options to install in walls, or wooden or metal doors. Doggy doors intended for permanent installation often have two flaps to help insulate your home and prevent drafts. If you have other household pets, consider whether they should have access to the outdoors before installing a doggy door. If you have neighborhood strays or wild animals, you should also consider whether they may be able to find their way into your house. If you're worried about what animals may be able to enter or exit your home through the doggy door, consider one that requires a certain type of collar tag in order to be unlocked. These types of doors will remain locked at all times unless an animal with a special tag approaches. This will allow your dog to come and go as he pleases, but your indoor cat and the neighborhood raccoon will stay where they belong.

Remember, when you allow your Australian Cattle Dog more space, you're trusting him to make the right decisions regarding your home and his own safety. More space indoors may mean more room for messes. If your puppy is able to escape from his playpen, he may be able to get into serious trouble before you come home. Before installing a doggy door, you should also make sure your yard is secure and that there is nothing dangerous your dog can get into or eat while he's outside unsupervised. If you think any wild animals that could endanger your dog might be able to get into your yard, you may want to reconsider allowing your dog unsupervised access to the outdoors.

CHAPTER 7
Socializing with People and Animals

Importance of Good Socialization

"Start young. ACD's are super smart and need to learn right away that people, in general, are good. With ACD's you need to show them that whoever/whatever your introducing them to is safe. If it's another dog, start by petting the other dog and showing your pup/dog that you like this other dog. Your ACD will then realize that they don't need to protect you from the other dog and will then be friendly and want to play."

Kacy VanDuinen
Triple M Corgis (and Cattle Dogs)

Photo Courtesy of
Kelsey George

One of the greatest benefits of good socialization is that you'll be able to confidently take your Australian Cattle Dog anywhere, knowing that you can trust him to behave and leave a good impression on everyone he meets. This enables you to take your dog to the vet, groomer, or boarding facility, knowing that he can handle it without undue stress. You'll also be able to take your

HELPFUL TIP
Socialization is Crucial

Australian Cattle Dogs tend to be snappy with people or animals they don't know. Give them plenty of exposure to other people and animals when they're puppies to help them be friendlier. Otherwise, you may end up with a dog who snaps at everybody but you and your family.

dog with you on vacation, to work, or while you run errands. A properly socialized dog will be welcome at any dog-friendly establishment. Traveling with a confident, well-socialized dog will enable you to focus on the task at hand, rather than on what your dog is doing and how he might react to his environment. The more time your dog can spend with you, the happier he'll be.

When you begin working on socialization, it's essential to focus on exposing your Australian Cattle Dog to as many positive experiences as possible. This means introducing him to new people, pets, animals, and locations. However, it's important to be aware of your dog's body language at all times and beware of any situation in which your puppy feels uncomfortable or overwhelmed. During this important stage of your dog's training and development, it's important to avoid negative experiences. Even a single negative experience can leave a lasting impression on your puppy and it can take serious training and commitment to overcome that trauma. Dog parks may seem like a wonderful place to introduce your puppy to new people and dogs, but they are actually quite dangerous. Owners typically take their dogs to the park to let them run off their energy, often paying little attention to them once they've unclipped the leash. Veterinary clinics see dogs nearly every day who have been injured in fights at the dog park. Even if your puppy isn't physically injured, the chaotic energy of the dog park may be overwhelming. You want to avoid any situation that could cause your dog to develop anxiety around new pets or people. Rather than the unstructured environment of a dog park, consider setting up playdates with friends and family with dogs in a quieter, more controlled atmosphere.

Behavior Around Other Dogs

"ACD's seem to enjoy control and they can have a tenancy to be the 'fun police'. They generally do not tolerate other socially rude dogs and do not do well at dog parks. Some cattle dogs have trouble with bicycles and joggers when out on a walk. The herding instinct may surface, making the ACD want to control the motion."

Alison Whittington
Hardtack Australian Cattle Dogs

Australian Cattle Dogs are typically confident and friendly with other dogs. However, it's not uncommon for them to be somewhat standoffish around new dogs, especially during the early stages of socialization. The more canine friends your dog makes, the less likely he is to be uncomfortable during introductions. It's important to introduce your dog to as many different kinds of dogs as possible, without risking any bad experiences. If you have friends, family, neighbors, or co-workers with pets, try setting up a playdate or scheduling a walk together. Dogs come in such a wide range of shapes and sizes that it's not uncommon for puppies to develop anxiety around certain breeds. For instance, if your Australian Cattle Dog has only spent time with small dogs, he may be fearful or uncertain the first time he meets a Great Dane.

Photo Courtesy of
Max Wood

Photo Courtesy of
Whitney Doherty

Understanding your dog's body language is key to ensuring that he has a good experience meeting new dogs. When two friendly dogs meet, their body language is typically quite relaxed and confident. Their tails may be wagging, and their ears will be perked up with interest, but not intensity. They'll sniff each other with a relaxed posture. If they're feeling playful, one dog may bow down to encourage the other to play. If either dog begins the introduction with a stiff body, head in the air, and ears pinned back, you can be sure that things are about to go south. Dogs with anxious body language may wag their tails, but it's not the relaxed wag of a new friend. Aggressive body language is not the only thing you should be looking out for, as fear can escalate into aggression quickly. Fearful dogs may cower or tuck their tails between their hind legs. Licking lips and showing teeth are also signs of extreme submission. Some dogs may even urinate out of fear. If either your Australian Cattle Dog or the dog you're introducing him to displays anything

Photo Courtesy of Tiffany Hughes

other than confident, relaxed body language, you need to be ready to remove both animals from the situation.

Remember to stay relaxed when introducing your Australian Cattle Dog to any new dog. Your puppy will be able to sense any tension in your body and he may believe that there is a reason to be worried about this stranger. Try not to grip the leash too tightly. As long as you keep an eye on your dog's body language and stay aware of your surroundings, you won't need to worry. Most of the time, you can expect your dog to walk away from an introduction with a new friend.

Never leave your Australian Cattle Dog alone with a dog that you don't know well, especially during the early stages of your dog's socialization. Accidents can happen in the blink of an eye and the only way you can prevent them is with proper supervision. Just because your dog is social and friendly does not mean that every dog you introduce him to will be the same. If you ever have any doubts about whether an introduction is going to go well, it's best to err on the side of caution and remove your dog from the situation.

Ways to Socialize Your Australian Cattle Dog with Other Pets

Socializing your dog with a variety of different types of animals will make him a more confident dog no matter where you take him. Try to introduce your Australian Cattle to as many different types of animals as possible. If you have no other pets in the home, ask friends and family members if you can introduce your puppy to their animals.

Before introducing your Australian Cattle Dog to other pets, it's important to remember that they are a herding breed and may try to nip at or herd new animals. This instinct is great when introducing your dog to livestock, but it's not ideal around other people's pets. Keep a close eye on any interaction with a new pet until you feel confident that no one will get hurt.

As with introducing your puppy to other dogs, it's essential that you prevent your puppy from becoming overwhelmed by the experience. Stay calm and closely supervise any interaction. If your dog, or the other animal, exhibits any sign of anxiety, fear, or aggression, separate the two immediately. You may need to try introducing them more slowly. Some animals, such as cats, may not appreciate enthusiastic puppies jumping all over them, so you need to be ready to intervene quickly if necessary.

When you first introduce your Australian Cattle Dog to new animals, it's a good idea to keep him on a leash. It's best if you can also safely restrain the other animal. Accidents can happen in the blink of an eye, but they can be stopped quickly or even prevented if both animals are properly restrained.

Never leave your Australian Cattle Dog unsupervised with new pets until you can accurately predict their behavior. This is especially important if there is a significant size difference between the animals. It may take several weeks or even months until you know that the animals are trustworthy enough to be left alone together. In some cases, pets may never be able to be left together unsupervised. For example, if your Australian Cattle Dog has a particularly high prey drive, you may find it difficult to trust him around smaller pets such as cats, rabbits, or chickens.

Photo Courtesy of Misty Bland

Properly Greeting New People

It's not uncommon for Australian Cattle Dogs to be aloof around strangers, so don't be surprised if your new puppy doesn't enthusiastically greet new people. Some dogs may be more willing to make friends than others, but it's important to let your dog introduce himself on his own terms. Shoving him into the arms of a stranger may only make him nervous or fearful, so let him approach new people on his own. If your dog is particularly hesitant to say hello, you can also have the new person offer him a few treats to show that they mean him no harm.

If your new dog is nervous around new people, it's important to let him take his time in saying hello, but you should not allow him to display any signs of fearfulness or aggression. Barking or growling should be corrected immediately. If your puppy seems anxious, it's best to ignore his discomfort rather than attempt to comfort him. By comforting him, you are only reinforcing his belief that he should be uncomfortable around strangers. If you allow your dog to be fearful or aggressive around new people, his behavior will only escalate as he grows. Eventually, you'll have a dog with major behavioral problems that may take years to correct. Teaching your puppy the correct way to greet strangers is the best way to prevent future problems.

As with any desired behavior, you should encourage your Australian Cattle Dog with positive reinforcement. When your puppy politely greets someone new, be sure to praise him and let him know he's doing well. Having new people offer your dog treats will also encourage him to say hello and let him know that strangers are nothing to be afraid of. Once your dog realizes that new people are new sources of treats and affection, he'll be more confident about making new friends.

Australian Cattle Dogs and Children

Dogs and children can be the best of friends, but only with thorough preparation and supervision. If both the dog and the kids are taught to act responsibly, the opportunity for a beautiful friendship can develop. However, if you aren't careful, accidents can happen. Enthusiastic children can easily hurt or scare a puppy, who might respond by biting. Until you are confident that your Australian Cattle Dog and children are trustworthy enough to spend time together, supervision is essential.

Before you bring your new dog home, sit down with your children and explain the rules of interacting with dogs. If you wait until you bring the pup-

Photo Courtesy of
Michael and Sheila Palmeter

py home, your kids may be too excited to focus on what you're telling them. Young children often treat animals as if they are toys, not realizing that they can injure a real dog. Explain to the children how they should handle the dog and try to discourage them from picking the puppy up. Once you're sure that they understand the rules, then you can introduce them to their new family member.

The bond between children and their new dog must be cultivated with care, so don't be afraid to intervene and separate them if necessary. Emotions can escalate quickly, so if you feel that either the children or the puppy is getting too wild, feel free to separate them and try again when everyone has calmed down. At first, you may only be able to have them together for a few moments at a time, but as they get used to each other you can increase the duration of their play sessions.

As herding dogs, Australian Cattle Dogs frequently incorporate their ancestral purpose into their play sessions. It's common for herding dogs to try to herd children around, especially when they get too rambunctious. They may try to nip at the children's heels to get them to move in the right direction. Even small nips can break the skin of a small child, so try to discourage any herding. Even if you intend to work livestock with your dog in the future, he should learn which creatures he is allowed to herd and which he is not.

Never leave your kids with your Australian Cattle Dog unattended. Accidents can happen in the blink of an eye and proper supervision is the only way to prevent them. Likely, neither the children nor the dog will hurt each other on purpose, but things can escalate quickly during rowdy play sessions. To prevent injury to both child and dog, it's best to keep an eye on everyone until you have a better understanding of the dynamics of their relationship.

CHAPTER 8

Australian Cattle Dogs and Your Other Pets

Introducing Your New Puppy to Other Animals

"Keep introductions to other pets to one at a time initially, so that the pup is not overwhelmed. Socialization with other pets as well as people should include animals and people outside the family (once the pup is fully vaccinated) to insure that your dog will be a confident, friendly and reliable companion in any situation you two may encounter."

Gwen Shepperson
Buffalo Creek Cattle Dogs

Photo Courtesy of Matilda Kitcker

Introducing your Australian Cattle Dog to a variety of other animals will help him become a confident and trustworthy companion. When first introducing your puppy to a new animal, it may be best to allow the animals to view each other at a distance. Allowing each animal their space and the opportunity to approach each other according to their own comfort levels will help reduce stress during the meeting. As they get closer, if either the dog or the new animal show signs of anxiety, increase the distance between them and try again once they relax. If

Photo Courtesy of
Mary Evans

both animals seem comfortable in each other's presence, you can let them meet face to face.

As with introducing your puppy to other dogs and pets, safety must always be your priority. When meeting any new animal, your Australian Cattle Dog should always be on a leash and the other animal should be safely restrained. With larger animals, such as horses, it may be helpful to keep them behind a fence. This way they can walk away if they feel uncomfortable with the dog, but they can't hurt him. If the other animal can be safely restrained with a halter or leash, it's a good idea to do so. Restraining each animal will give you the ability to separate them quickly should things go awry. Without proper restraint, one or both animals can become seriously injured. Introducing unrestrained animals also presents the opportunity for you to become injured trying to separate fighting animals or trying to rescue one from the other.

Photo Courtesy of
Afton Trout

Supervision is essential no matter what type of animal you're introducing your new dog to. With larger animals, such as goats, sheep, or horses, you must be cautious about your Australian Cattle Dog's herding instinct. If left alone with livestock, your dog may try to chase them, which could result in an injury to either your dog or the other animals. If you are raising a working dog, or have an interest in competitive herding, it's best to work with a trainer to hone your dog's natural instincts, rather than just let him run wild and harass livestock. Remember, supervision is more than just being present while the animals interact. You must closely monitor their body language for any signs of anxiety, fear, or aggression. Accidents can happen quickly, so never leave your dog alone with any animal until you know them both well enough to predict their behavior.

Pack Mentality

Dogs naturally find comfort living in a group setting with a well-structured hierarchy. They are social animals and find comfort within the rules and limitations of their natural group order. Most dogs would prefer to follow than lead, but they are willing to lead if no other leader is present in their group. This is true in both a natural pack setting as well as a household of humans. Your dog's individual personality will dictate how easily he is willing to follow the rules. Some dogs are more dominant than others, so you may need to work harder to earn your position of pack leader. Regardless of how many dogs live in your home, it's important to set clear boundaries. If you allow your dog to live without rules, he may become unmanageable or even potentially dangerous. By bringing an Australian Cattle Dog into your home, you are accepting the responsibility of providing him with a loving home and strict household rules.

It's crucial that you begin implementing your rules the moment you bring your dog home. It can be easy to let an adorable puppy get away with certain behaviors, but that just means you'll be spending more time as he grows correcting your mistakes. Behaviors such as jumping up on people, refusing to get off furniture, or ignoring your commands will only escalate as time goes on. Resource guarding behaviors should not be tolerated under any circumstances. Do not allow your dog to act aggressively when you or your other pets come near his food, toys, or bed. All of these behaviors are relatively easy to correct in their early stages, but they have the potential to become difficult to fix and dangerous if they aren't dealt with early on. If you find yourself struggling to correct your dog and establish your

Photo Courtesy of Glenna Bochtler

position as pack leader, don't be afraid to consult a professional trainer as soon as possible.

Remember, in a pack setting in the wild, the leader is always the first to eat. He sleeps where he wants to, and he never moves out of the way when another dog approaches. In your own home, it's your responsibility to emulate this behavior. You must set boundaries for your dog and enforce them as needed. Never kick, hit, or yell at your dog. This will only teach him to be afraid of you and it's unlikely to alter the behavior you're trying to correct. In the wild, dogs correct each other with nips, nudges, and growls. Instead of growling, teach your dog the meaning of "no" and use confident body language to let your dog know who's in charge. At feeding time, teach your dog that he can't eat until you say so. Have him sit and wait patiently while you set the bowl down. Instead of allowing him to eat the moment the bowl touches the floor, ask him to wait a few moments before releasing him. Likewise, be sure that you're the first to walk through any doorway. If your dog tries to rush past you, have him sit quietly while you go through, releasing him once you're on the other side. As a pack leader, you have the right to choose where you want to rest, so if your dog is sitting in your favorite chair, don't be afraid to ask him to move. Being a calm, assertive leader will help you maintain a well-behaved and stable pack.

Fighting/Bad Behavior

"Nipping at other dogs, usually seen while playing or when new dogs meet your ACD and they are directing their attention to a new dog that hasn't yet determined pecking order. Proper correction is necessary to avoid fighting and to train them to redirect their urge to nip; this may require much patience and possibly the help of a professional."

Kelsey Bolton
Flintlock Farms

Aggressive behavior should be discouraged from the first sign. Even a small growl, or something as simple as pushing another dog away from their food bowl, could escalate into more serious behavior if you don't correct it. If your dog's aggression escalates into an actual fight, one or both dogs could become seriously injured. If the other dog is significantly smaller, it could even be killed. Australian Cattle Dogs aren't large dogs, but they have strong with powerful jaws. If you see your dog acting aggressively toward another dog, distract him by clapping loudly or stomping. Once you have his attention, call him away from the situation. Redirect his focus by asking him to perform a few simple commands such as sit or down. By making him focus on you rather than the other dog, you are diffusing the situation and hopefully preventing a fight.

Aggressive behavior can be incredibly difficult to correct, so it's best to prevent it from developing in the first place, if possible. In order to prevent aggression, you need to figure out why your dog is acting a certain way. If you don't know what's triggering your dog's behavior, you'll never be able to prevent him from acting out. Think about specific situations in which your dog acted aggressively and what each had in common. Managing your dog's environment is key to managing his behavior, so you need to determine

*Photo Courtesy of
Nicole McKenna*

what the cause of a problem is so you can remove it or manage it appro-priately. If you notice your dog has become aggressive toward other dogs over toys or food, you may need to remove the toys and feed the animals separately until you're able to control the situation better. Managing your dog's environment is key in managing his behavior, so you need to deter-mine what the cause is so you can remove it or deal with it appropriately.

If your Australian Cattle Dog's aggression does escalate into a fight, it's important to break the fight up with as little risk to yourself and the dogs as possible. Never grab one or both dogs. In the heat of the moment, they may not realize it's you grabbing them and they could easily turn around and bite you. Depending on the severity of the fight, you may need to try a few options to get the dogs to separate themselves. Loud noises are one of the more effective options. This is the one instance in which it's okay to yell at your dog. Yelling, clapping, stomping, or even banging metal food bowls together may enough to distract the dogs from the fight. Spraying or dump-ing water on the dogs also works well. If you have a blanket large enough to cover both dogs, you can also try tossing that over them. Once the dogs are separated, take hold of the aggressor and remove him immediately. If you can't distract the dogs, you must separate them in a way that prioritizes your own safety. Decide which dog is more aggressive and grab him by the hind legs. Pull him away from the other dog either by backing up or swinging him to the side. You must keep the momentum to prevent him from being able to turn around to bite you. Once you have the animals separated, restrain them immediately to prevent the fight from starting again.

Aggression is a serious behavior problem that must be dealt with as soon as possible. Recognizing when things have gotten out of your control is the first step in solving the problem. The sooner you are able to seek professional help, the more likely it is that you'll be able to prevent your dog from getting hurt or hurting another animal or human. If possible, seek the help of a professional trainer or behaviorist at the first sign of aggression.

Raising Multiple Puppies from the Same Litter

Raising your Australian Cattle Dog alongside one or more littermates may seem like an excellent idea, especially if you have no other pets in your home. However, you need to carefully consider the pros and cons before bringing home multiple puppies.

On the positive side, your puppies will have a friend to keep him company when you're away from home. The adjustment of moving into a new home will be less stressful for the puppies if they're coming with one of their littermates, with whom they've bonded. You'll never have to worry about being too tired after a long day at work to play with your dog, because he has had a playmate with him the entire time. You also won't have to worry about the puppies getting along as they've known each other since birth.

However, there are a few drawbacks to raising multiple puppies from the same litter. One puppy requires a lot of time and dedication to their training. With each additional puppy, you'll need to devote even more time and effort to teaching your dogs to become responsible citizens. Having bonded littermates can be great, but if you ever need to separate them, they may become insecure and anxious without each other. Bad habits are also multiplied when you have one or more dogs learning them together.

If you do decide to bring home more than one Australian Cattle Dog, you'll need to dedicate extra time to ensuring that each puppy develops as an individual, rather than as part of a pair or group. Be sure to take each puppy out alone for individual training and socialization. This way, the dogs can gain confidence either being out on their own or staying home alone.

Individual work is essential, but it's important to train them as a group as well. Managing two or more puppies who have only been trained separately can be difficult, so you need to teach them to walk politely as a group and interact with others in a calm and friendly manner. If you aren't sure you're ready to train multiple puppies at the same time, but you'd like to have more than one dog, consider adopting an additional puppy once the first one is a little more mature and further along in his training.

Options if Your Pets Don't Get Along

It's not uncommon for pets not to get along during the first weeks of living together. Some pets may need more time to adjust to the change, especially if they've lived alone for most of their life. Don't rush the relationship and certainly don't rush into any serious decisions regarding what to do with either pet. It can take weeks or months before some pets can tolerate each other. Remember, the more time you're willing to commit to working with your pets, the more likely they are to get along.

However, if you've dedicated the time and effort necessary to socializing your pets with each other and they just don't seem to get along, you may have a serious decision to make. The idea of giving up a beloved member of the family can be distressing, but you do have another option. Pets

Photo Courtesy of
Dominique Copelin

that don't get along can often live in the same household as long as they are kept separate. It can take a lot of time and energy to keep them separated and ensure that they receive equal amounts of care and affection, but it can be done. However, it's important to remember that you must be committed to doing this for the entirety of your pets' lives. This may mean a decade or more of managing two or more separate pets. You'll need to make sure their safety and well-being is a priority, which can be difficult and time-consuming. You must also take your pets' quality of life into consideration and decide whether this is really the best option for them.

HELPFUL TIP
Make Introductions Slowly

Australian Cattle Dogs were bred to bite cattle, not socialize with other dogs. Introduce your new Cattle Dog to your other pets slowly and monitor everybody's body language. Australian Cattle Dogs can get along with other pets, but it can be a slower process than with other breeds.

If you can't see yourself managing your pets in separate situations for the rest of their lives, you may want to consider finding another home for one of them. Some pets just prefer to be the only animal in a home, and that's perfectly fine. Others may just feel more comfortable in a different environment. Giving up a beloved pet is a heartbreaking decision, but it's often the best choice. As a pet owner, it's your responsibility to make the right choices regarding your pets' happiness and well-being.

CHAPTER 9
Physical and Mental Exercise

"Find the length and type of exercise that keeps them from being destructive and bored. A tired cattle dog is a good cattle dog. Not only will they need physical stimulation, but mental as well. They love to learn, teach them tricks or get them involved with outside activities like 'Barn hunt' competitions, agility, dock diving or obedience. There are endless opportunities and programs to get involved with your dog no matter your activity level or schedule that will give your dog a job, socialization and exercise."

Kelsey Bolton
Flintlock Farms

Photo Courtesy of
Karacel Hayman

Exercise Requirements

"Let them run until they can't run anymore. They are the greatest retrievers ever bred. Soft Frisbees like the Kong disk or others, tennis balls, anything they can go get and bring back. Sticks work fine too. And remember, when they bring it to you they did you a favor, be polite and thank them."

James C Beel
ACD Breeder

Physical exercise is essential to the overall well-being of your Australian Cattle Dog. Without enough exercise, dogs can quickly become overweight. Overweight dogs are more likely to develop arthritis, heart disease, and diabetes. As their mobility decreases due to excess weight, if their calorie intake is not adjusted accordingly, this can lead to further weight gain. The Australian Cattle Dog is an active breed, so the more opportunities you can give your dog to run or play, the better. Most dogs will require between 30 and 60 minutes of hard, physical exertion each day. Of course, if your Australian Cattle Dog is a healthy adult, he is certainly capable of more.

Mental stimulation, which is discussed further later on in the chapter, is just as important. If dogs don't receive enough mental stimulation, they may become bored and seek out ways to entertain themselves. They may also try to escape to seek out more interesting environments. Short training sessions one or more times per day are a great way to challenge your dog and prevent boredom.

For young puppies, seniors, or dogs with physical limitations, the amount and type of exercise will vary according to age and overall health. Too much exercise can cause permanent damage to a growing puppy's bones and joints, so it's best to limit a puppy's exercise to short play sessions and brief walks. As your dog ages, you may need to adjust the length of his walks, or simply reduce the intensity of his exercise sessions to accommodate sore joints and muscles. For dogs with physical limitations, mental exercise is even more important. Often, a dog's body slows down much earlier than his mind, so keeping your dog mentally active is essential.

Different Types of Exercise to Try

"Learning to play fetch and long walks are key. Each pup is different, but each needs ample exercise daily."

Brett Spader
Spader Kennels

Herding is one of the best types of exercise for an Australian Cattle Dog. Not only is it physically challenging, but it requires your dog to make independent decisions about how to move livestock. Equally effective is training your Aussie to herd sheep, goats, and even ducks.

If you live in an urban area, you may want to try a relatively new dog sport called treibball. Treibball offers your dog the benefits of traditional herding without the hassle of actual livestock. Handler and dog work together off-leash to drive eight fitness-type balls into a goal in under seven minutes. Once all the balls are in the goal, the dog must lie down in front of the goal in order to complete the round. Treibball can be played indoors or out, and competitions are held by the American Treibball Association across the country.

Photo Courtesy of
Amanda Willman

*Photo Courtesy of
Amy Sanderell*

Obedience is another sport in which Australian Cattle Dogs can thrive. Dogs must perform a variety of tasks including heeling, sitting, retrieving dumbbells, and staying in a sit, down, or stand. Different levels of difficulty allow dogs of all ages and experience levels a chance to compete. Lower levels are performed on-leash and the challenges are relatively easy, such as heeling, sitting, and lying down. More advanced levels are performed off-leash and dogs are asked to perform more difficult tasks, such as lengthy stays and retrieving dumbbells, and stay for longer periods of time. If traditional obedience competitions sound boring, you may also want to consider rally obedience, a faster-paced competition where similar tasks are performed, but in a quicker sequence. Signs are posted around the course instructing handlers and dogs to perform 10-20 tasks as quickly and accurately as possible.

Agility is a great way to test your communication and exercise your dog's body and mind. Agility competitions are high-energy events that involve a handler and dog working together off-leash to overcome a variety

Photo Courtesy of
Glenna Bochtler

of obstacles such as jumps, tunnels, and weave poles. The fastest dog with the most accurate round wins. Competitors are divided into groups by size, so smaller breeds are not forced to compete with larger breeds.

HELPFUL TIP
Exercise Prevents Destruction

Australian Cattle Dogs are intelligent and energetic. If they don't get enough physical or mental stimulation, they're likely to tear your home apart when they're alone. If your Cattle Dog is causing chaos when you're away, try giving her more exercise and puzzle toys to keep her mind engaged.

If agility sounds exciting, but you'd rather not run around the course with your dog, consider flyball, especially if your dog loves to fetch. Dogs compete as part of a team of four, racing over a series of hurdles to pounce onto a wooden box that releases a tennis ball into their mouth. Once they have the ball, they run back over the hurdles to the start line, where the next dog on the team is waiting. After the first dog crosses the line, the second is released, and so forth until all four dogs have finished.

If your Australian Cattle Dog is a strong jumper and swimmer, you may want to give dock diving a try. Dock diving is an off-leash sport that rewards the dog who can jump the furthest into a pool of water. To encourage dogs to jump as far as possible, dogs are given a running start and a buoyant toy is tossed out into the water for them to retrieve. It's an excellent way to stay cool in the summer and keep your dog fit.

Canicross is a great option if you're looking for a sport where you get as much exercise as your dog. Although most popular in Europe, it's gaining popularity around the world. Dogs typically wear a harness, similar to those used on sled dogs, which is attached by a bungee leash to a harness worn around your waist. The goal is to have your dog pull you along as you run. Races are held across the country, usually on well-maintained trails. Distances and difficulty of terrain vary, but much like typical foot races, the fastest team wins.

Importance of Mental Exercise

"Are you smart enough to be owned by an Australian Cattle Dog? ACD's thrive on mental stimulation even more than physical exercise and if they become bored.....get ready for a mess!"

Alison Whittington
Hardtack Australian Cattle Dogs

A bored dog is nearly guaranteed to be a badly behaved dog, so in order to teach your Australian Cattle Dog to be a responsible member of your household, you need to make sure you're exercising his mind as well as his body. Boredom usually manifests in destructive behaviors, so if you notice your dog has begun chewing up furniture, shoes, toys, or pillows, you may need to focus more on mental exercise. Even if your dog has had hours of physical exercise, he still needs to be able to use his mind. Thankfully, mental exercise can be quite exhausting, so you won't need to spend quite as much time on this. You may notice that after an hour-long walk your dog is still as energetic as ever, but after a 15-minute training session, he's ready for a nap. This is especially true with puppies and older dogs.

Photo Courtesy of Gina Burroughs

If your Australian Cattle Dog is young, old, or has any physical limitations that make physical exercise difficult, you may need to focus more on mental stimulation. Sports such as scent work, tracking, or even treibball can all be done at a slower pace and emphasize the mind rather than the body. You may also want to try offering your dog puzzle toys or snuffle mats to keep him entertained at home. Dogs of any age are capable of learning a variety of tricks, so you can tailor your training sessions to accommodate your dog's special needs. The American Kennel Club now offers a Trick Dog competition, where dogs compete by performing five to ten tricks. Many of the tricks required for competition are low-impact and possible for young and old dogs alike.

Photo Courtesy of Hayley Whitney

The most important aspect of mental stimulation is to keep your sessions short. Mental exercise can be tiresome and if you work your dog past the point of exhaustion, you both may become frustrated. While training, you need to closely monitor your Australian Cattle Dog's body language to make sure he's still focused on his work. If you notice his attention drifting or he seems to be struggling, it may be best to quit and try again later. There is no ideal length for a training session, so if your dog gets tired at around seven minutes, you may want to quit at five minutes. Training sessions are of no value if they leave a negative impression on your dog, so keep them short and sweet.

Tips for Keeping Your Australian Cattle Dog Occupied

"You must engage the mind of an ACD. There are many fun enrichment activities that you can provide your dog or pup. Kibble puzzles, playing 'hide and treat', training for different dog sports or simply teaching a 'silly pet trick' in your kitchen. I would also add that finding the time and place for a long nature walk will do you both wonders."

Alison Whittington
Hardtack Australian Cattle Dogs

One of the most popular ways to keep your dog busy is to get creative with how you feed him. Australian Cattle Dogs love to use their mind, especially when allowed to do so independently. Many owners have found success with hiding food around their house or yard. Ask your dog to wait in his crate or in another room while you hide pieces of kibble or treats behind furniture, on shelves, in the grass, or even in plain sight. Once you've hidden all the food, release your dog and encourage him to start looking by using a command such as "Find it." After a few repetitions, your dog will understand what you're asking him to do and will likely get to work right away.

Photo Courtesy of Jennifer Todd

Another option is to hide food inside of a plastic or wooden puzzle toy. Your local pet store or favorite online retailer likely has a selection of different puzzle toys. The toys may have knobs, cups, sliding doors, or flaps that your dog needs to manipulate with either his nose or paws to reach the treats inside. Australian Cattle Dogs can figure out a puzzle rather quickly so you may want to have a few on hand to mix it up. Offering a different challenge each day will keep your dog interested. You can also try purchasing puzzles with different levels of difficulty to further challenge your dog. Just be sure to keep a close eye on your dog to make sure he doesn't break or chew off pieces of the toys in his excitement to reach the food.

Another popular method of keeping dogs busy is hiding food inside of rubber chew toys, such as Kong toys. These toys are made of a tough, rubber material and have a hollow center that can be filled with treats or food. They come in a variety of sizes and densities to accommodate dogs of all sizes and jaw strengths. Depending on your dog's needs and interests, you may want to try stuffing the toy with kibble or canned food, vegetables, or even peanut butter. At first, your dog may chase the toy around using only his mouth to get the food out. With experience, he may learn to hold the toy with his paw while he licks the food out, but you can always increase the challenge with more difficult to reach foods. You can also try freezing the contents of the toy to increase the level of difficulty and keep your dog cool on hot summer days. It's a good idea to buy a few toys so you can fill them all at once and store them in the freezer to dispense at a moment's notice.

Snuffle mats are another option that encourages your dog to forage for his food. They're flat mats that are typically made of fleece, or another easy-to-clean fabric cut into long strips. Snuffle mats can be purchased in store and online or you can make your own at home using simple instructions found on the internet. Either way, they're quite inexpensive. To use, take a small handful of kibble or dry treats and sprinkle them over the mat. Ruffle the strips with your hand to hide the treats deeper in the mat. Most snuffle mats are machine washable.

Even for active adult dogs a few extra calories may not seem like much, but if you offer extra treats every day, in any form, they can add up. To help keep your dog's waistline under control, consider using a portion of his daily kibble. Some owners even feed their dog's entire meal using some type of toy or game. You can also try using low-calorie options such as vegetables as treats. Fruit tends to be higher in sugar, so use sparingly.

CHAPTER 10
Training Your Australian Cattle Dog

"ACD's are quite mischievous and they tend to think 'outside the box'. They are happy to comply with your demands, but often think they know a better way to get it done."

Alison Whittington
Hardtack Australian Cattle Dogs

Photo Courtesy of Ashlyn Talley

Photo Courtesy of Cassy Moore

Clear Expectations

"Be firm with your ACD. Do not let their occasional stubbornness trick you into thinking they are too difficult to handle. Stay consistent! Reward them when they are doing the right thing, they thrive when they are pleasing you. Also be firm with corrections, their desire to please drives them to behave in a way that causes positive attention from their human."

Kelsey Bolton
Flintlock Farms

When you begin training your Australian Cattle Dog, be realistic about your expectations. If you only work with your dog once a week, he's not likely to progress in his training very fast. Daily training is much more effective. It can be helpful to set small goals, for each training session or each day, to help you stay on track.

Be sure to set your dog up for success with every training session. Clear and consistent communication will help you get your point across, so be sure that you are using the same commands each time. If you're not consistent in your training or your commands, your dog is likely to become confused and frustrated. This frustration will carry over to your next training sessions, where he will be less eager to focus on you.

Never ask more of your dog than he is capable of at any given moment in his training. If your dog consistently responds to your commands in your kitchen, but tends to lose focus in the back yard, don't take him to the local park or a café and expect him to listen to you. Training must always be done in small steps. Otherwise, your dog will become overwhelmed and confused. Instead of presenting him with a situation you know he can't yet handle, avoid difficult situations until you're more confident in his training. If your goal is to have your dog sit quietly next to you outside the local coffee shop, work your way toward this by slowly increasing the challenges in his training, rather than attempting the task all at once.

To make the most out of every training session, you should always end on a good note. Even if things didn't go as planned, you can still leave a positive impression on your dog by returning to a task that he knows well. If you were working on your recall and he seemed unfocused or you both got frustrated, try asking him to sit or lie down a few times before ending the session. This way, you can reward him for doing a good job with something he knows well, instead of ending the session with a feeling of frustration. You can always return to the original task at a later time, once you've both had a chance to unwind.

Photo Courtesy of
Regan Miller

Photo Courtesy of
Tiffany Hughes

Operant Conditioning Basics

Operant conditioning is based on the idea that if a specific behavior is followed by either a reward or a punishment, the learner will either be more or less willing to repeat the behavior in the future. Operant conditioning was originally promoted by the American behaviorist and psychologist B.F. Skinner, who believed that if a behavior is followed by a positive experience, known as "reinforcers," then the learner is more likely to repeat the behavior. Similarly, if a behavior is followed by a negative experience, the learner will be discouraged from repeating the behavior.

Positive reinforcement is one of the most well-known training methods for dogs because of its efficacy. Dogs learn well with positive reinforcement, especially when food and attention are used as reinforcers. Rewards typically consist of either primary reinforcements, such as food, or secondary reinforcements, such as praise. Unfortunately, accidental positive reinforcement can also be used in the development of bad habits. For instance, if your dog knocks over the trash can and is rewarded with a tasty buffet of leftovers, he's likely to knock the trash can over again in the future. Part of being an effective trainer is managing not only a dog's behavior, but his environment as well.

Negative reinforcement is used less commonly in dog training than positive reinforcement, but it can be an effective training tool when used correctly. To be clear: negative reinforcement and punishment are not the same thing. Negative reinforcement does not harm your dog, it simply encourages him to repeat certain behaviors due to the removal of an unpleasant stimulus, such as gentle pressure from your hand or the leash. For example, when leash training your dog, you need to teach him to give in to the pressure of the leash in order to follow you where you want to walk. To accomplish this, you put gentle pressure on the leash in the direction you want your dog to move. Not enough to physically move him forward, but enough to prevent him from moving backward. Eventually, the dog will move forward and when he does, all pressure on the leash is immediately removed. After a few repetitions, the dog learns that moving with the leash, rather than against it, will prevent him from having any unpleasant pressure on his collar or harness.

Punishments are exactly what you might expect. When a behavior is followed by a negative response, the dog becomes less likely to repeat the behavior in the future. For example, if your Australian Cattle Dog has a habit of getting too close to the neighbor's cat, the cat may eventually swipe at him and scratch his nose. After a few scratches, your dog will learn not to stick his nose too close to the cat. The scratches on his nose are a punishment which will discourage him from repeating the behavior again.

Photo Courtesy of Libbi Watters

Primary Reinforcements—Food, Toys, Playtime

"ACDs tend to be easy to train once you understand their motivation. Many are treat motivated and thrive on creating movement, like working livestock or playing fetch."

Brett Spader
Spader Kennels

Primary reinforcements reward the dog on a biological level and are based on environmental responses that would affect a dog's behavior in the wild. All dogs are driven by the desire to seek food, water, and pleasure, so an effective dog trainer will use their dog's natural drives to their advantage.

One of the best ways to motivate your Australian Cattle Dog in a training session is to reward him with food or treats. As with humans, some dogs will eat nearly anything and enjoy it, while others may be pickier. Foods that your dog will choose to eat over all others are referred to as high-value foods. Trainers often use high-value foods only in training sessions to encourage their dogs to participate. Pickier dogs will be more motivated to focus with high-value foods, but if your dog is one that will happily gobble up anything, you may find success in using portions of his daily kibble as training treats.

Toys and play can also be effective rewards to reinforce your dog's behavior. Some dogs respond better to toys than others, so you may need to try a few. Toys and playtime reflect a dog's natural desire to hunt and chase prey. Squeaky toys mimic the sound of small prey animals, which is why many dogs enjoy biting and pouncing on them. Games like fetch mimic a dog's behavior when chasing down prey. In the wild, chasing and catching prey results in food, so it's natural for dogs to enjoy the process, even though in modern life it doesn't always end in food.

105

Secondary Reinforcements—Attention, Praise, Clickers

Secondary reinforcements must be taught as they are not naturally rewarding like primary reinforcements. Dogs must be taught through experience that secondary reinforcements mean that they've done a good job. Although many dogs enjoy attention and praise, they do not automatically know what "good boy" means, or what the sound of a clicker represents. In order for your dog to understand secondary reinforcements, you must build a connection between your primary and secondary reinforcements of choice. You can even focus solely on this connection for a few training sessions before you begin teaching your dog commands.

Attention and praise work well as rewards for many dogs, but some dogs don't thrive on attention so it may mean little to them initially. In order to teach your dog the value of verbal praise, come up with a marker word that you can use consistently in his training. Give your dog a treat as you say the marker word of your choice, such as "good" or "yes." After several repetitions, he'll understand that when he hears that word, he's going to get a treat. As he progresses, you can give him verbal praise and then hesitate a moment before giving him the treat. This way, you'll work toward relying more on secondary reinforcement.

If you would prefer not to use a marker word, you can also use a clicker in place of verbal praise. To teach your dog the value of the sound of the clicker, press the clicker and give a treat until your dog understands that the sound of the clicker means that food is coming. Again, you can eventually increase the time between the click and the food or use just a click as a reward every so often. Eventually, he'll learn that the clicker means he's done a good job even if he doesn't get a treat every time.

With enough practice, you can eventually use only secondary reinforcements in your training. However, unlike with primary reinforcements, the value of secondary reinforcements may decrease over time, so you may need to go back to using treats or toys to reward your dog on occasion. It may also be useful to go back to primary reinforcements when working on particularly difficult or confusing concepts to encourage your dog to stay focused and engaged.

Negative Reinforcement

Some trainers see little value in negative reinforcement, while others find it quite useful when used in combination with positive reinforcement. It's your duty as your dog's trainer to see what method he responds best to and use it responsibly. Remember, negative reinforcement encourages a dog to repeat a desired behavior by removing an un-

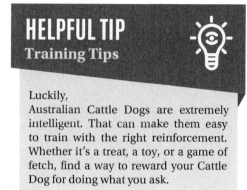

HELPFUL TIP
Training Tips

Luckily, Australian Cattle Dogs are extremely intelligent. That can make them easy to train with the right reinforcement. Whether it's a treat, a toy, or a game of fetch, find a way to reward your Cattle Dog for doing what you ask.

pleasant sensation. This is different from a punishment, which is when a behavior is followed with an unpleasant sensation, which will discourage the dog from repeating the behavior in the future. However, in order for negative reinforcement to be effective, your timing must be perfect. You must release the pressure on the dog the moment he responds appropriately. If you don't, the pressure becomes a punishment and you may inadvertently discourage him from repeating a desired behavior.

Negative reinforcement is an effective learning method, but it generally works best in combination with positive reinforcement. An example of proper negative reinforcement is used when teaching a dog to sit. As you give the verbal command "sit," put your hand above your dog's hip and place gentle pressure to encourage him to sit. Don't push him down into the sit, as this won't teach him anything. Instead, apply just enough pressure to encourage him to move away from it, but not so much that you physically move his body. The moment your dog lowers his hind end, release the pressure. At the moment of release, also reward your dog with positive reinforcement by praising him and giving him a treat. Eventually, your dog will realize that he can avoid the pressure on his hind end by sitting when given the verbal command.

Hiring a Trainer/Attending Classes

"These dogs want to have a job by nature as they are a working/herding breed that has been bred to control movement of others, originally cattle, by biting and herding. Teach your puppy when this is appropriate and when it is not permitted--redirect them with firm, fair, and consistent rules and training. Seek out a trainer if you are not successful on your own."

Gwen Shepperson
Buffalo Creek Cattle Dogs

Even if you've trained dogs in the past, working with a professional can be incredibly helpful. Even if your dog doesn't have any behavioral issues, trainers can help you meet your goals faster. Trainers can be especially helpful if you plan on competing with your dog.

Photo Courtesy of Melissa Lynch

Most trainers offer a variety of classes to suit different dogs at different levels in their training. You may consider either private or group lessons. If your dog has any behavioral problems, it may be best to do private sessions until you've both developed enough confidence to attend group training sessions. As for group lessons, you get the added benefit of socializing and working with your dog in a distracting environment. Although you won't have the full attention of the trainer as you would in a private lesson, you'll still be able ask questions and have your problems addressed.

If you're having problems with your dog, such as fear, aggression, or you just can't keep him focused, seek the advice of a trainer. Fearful and aggressive behavior can escalate quickly, so it's essential that you get in touch with a trainer or behaviorist as soon as possible, before someone gets hurt.

Owner Behavior

"ACD's are extremely loyal and protective. They are also super smart. When training an ACD be careful because they can learn bad habits just as quick as the good ones."

Kacy VanDuinen
Triple M Corgis (and Cattle Dogs)

One of the most important aspects of training your own dog is holding yourself accountable. If you aren't dedicated to your dog's education, your dog won't be either. Everyone has bad days, but you shouldn't let them affect your relationship with your dog. Be enthusiastic and committed to the training and your dog will be eager to learn every day.

If you're having difficulties in your training, you may want to take a moment and reflect on your own body language and behavior. Dogs are incredibly sensitive to their owners, so you may be affecting your dog in ways that you're unaware of. If you're tense or uncomfortable, you may be sending the wrong message to your dog. Remember to be the calm, confident leader your dog needs.

CHAPTER 11
Basic Commands

"This is a working breed and highly active, as well as highly intelligent. The saying goes 'a tired ACD is a good ACD', and it really is true! Make sure your dog gets enough physical exercise daily but also mental exercise as well--these dogs are eager to learn/please and can be taught to do just about anything. If you do not provide enough activity, they generally find ways to employ themselves - usually not positive!"

Gwen Shepperson
Buffalo Creek Cattle Dogs

Benefits of Proper Training

The mental and physical stimulation provided by regular training sessions are a great way to keep your Australian Cattle Dog's mind and body fit. Even sessions as short as 5-10 minutes can provide your dog with much needed mental and physical exercise. With regular training sessions, not only will your dog's manners improve, but he'll be much calmer and easier to manage. A calmer dog is also more likely to focus on you during your next training session.

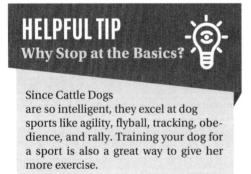

HELPFUL TIP
Why Stop at the Basics?

Since Cattle Dogs are so intelligent, they excel at dog sports like agility, flyball, tracking, obedience, and rally. Training your dog for a sport is also a great way to give her more exercise.

Another benefit of proper training is that you'll be able to take your dog anywhere and be able to trust him to behave himself. You'll be able to confidently take your Australian Cattle Dog with you on vacation or to run errands around town. With training and socialization, your dog will able to handle any situation with a calm and collected attitude.

Basic Commands

Regardless of whether you're raising a future working ranch dog or a family companion, there are a few basic commands that will make life with your Australian Cattle Dog easier. Commands such as sit, stay, and come are essential for any dog. In order to maintain your position as pack leader, you'll also need to teach your dog commands for getting off the furniture or dropping whatever he has in his mouth. A well-trained dog will also need to know how to walk politely on a leash without pulling. There's no limit to the number of commands you can teach your dog, but these are a few of the basics.

Sit

One of the first commands most trainers teach puppies is "sit." It's one of the easier commands for dogs to learn and most dogs, especially those as intelligent as Australian Cattle Dogs, pick up on it rather quickly. The sit command is also useful in teaching your dog patience and is the basis for many other commands such as stay. If your dog tends to get excited when meeting new people, the sit command is also an excellent way to teach him to wait patiently for attention, rather than jumping up on people.

Photo Courtesy of Emma O'Sullivan

To teach your puppy to sit, wave a treat in front of his nose to get his attention. Once he's focused on you and the treat, give him the verbal command "sit" and raise the treat above his head high enough that he can't quite reach it, but not so high that he tries to jump to get it. Most dogs learn rather quickly that they can look up better if they are sitting rather than standing. If necessary, add some negative reinforcement to your training by placing your hand above your puppy's hips and applying gentle pressure while you raise the treat with your other hand. The moment the dog begins to lower his hips, remove the pressure to reward him. Be sure to use plenty of praise to let your puppy know he's done a good job.

Stay

Photo Courtesy of Amanda Southwood

Teaching your Australian Cattle Dog the stay command will teach him patience and self-control. You can vary the difficulty of this command by increasing the time you ask your dog to stay, increasing the distance between yourself and your dog, and adding distractions. It's also a great skill for your dog to have if you plan on taking him out in public. You'll be able to ask your dog to stay while you run inside the coffee shop to order, knowing that he'll wait patiently for your return. Many trainers choose to differentiate between "stay" and "wait" in order to prevent confusion. Stay is generally used for longer periods of time and the dog is only released when the handler returns to the original position he or she was in when the dog was given the command. Wait is used for shorter time periods and the dog can be released from some distance away. For example, if you're working on your dog's recall, you may ask him to stay while you walk to the other side of the yard to call him over to you. Wait can also be used to ask your dog to practice patience while you set down his food bowl or gather your belongings to leave the house.

You may ask your dog to stay or wait while he's sitting, standing or lying down. In the early stages, many dogs may find it difficult to stay standing or lying down as they can be easily distracted from these positions, so the stay is best started from a sitting position. Ask your dog to sit and give him the verbal command "stay" or "wait," whichever you choose to use or work on. After just a second, if he holds his position, you can reward him. If he moves, simply return him to the sit position and begin again. You may only be able to get a second or two of staying at first, but with practice, you can build up to several minutes or longer.

Lie Down

If you plan on competing in any dog sports with your Australian Cattle Dog, he may be required to know how to lie down during competition, so it's essential that he understand this command. If your puppy is destined for life as a family companion it's still a useful command at vet clinics or in the car. You can also use lie down as the first step in tricks such as rolling over or crawling. If you've already taught your dog to sit, teaching him to lie down is quite simple.

As with teaching the sit command, luring with treats is the easiest way to teach your dog to lie down. From a sitting position, gain his attention with a treat and slowly lower the treat in front of him as you give the command "lie down." You may want to move the treat away from him a bit, just to give him room to lie down. Most dogs understand this quite easily and will not try to stand up, but if your dog gets excited about the treat, simply return him to the sitting position and try again. It's important that you only reward your dog for lying down completely. Many dogs will try to crouch, rather than lie down all the way, so only reward once his elbows are touching the ground.

Photo Courtesy of
Jessica Spall

Come

The recall, or "come," command, is one of the most important skills you can teach your dog. Not only will it make life in your home easier, but it may even save your dog's life if he ends up in a sticky situation. If you plan on having your dog off-leash, either in competition or just at the local park or hiking trail, a solid recall is essential. The easiest method of teaching your dog to come involves two handlers, so if you have a friend or family who can help you, it might make your training session easier.

It's best to begin your training in a familiar area that won't distract your puppy too much, such as your yard or even inside your house. If you aren't comfortable having your puppy off-leash, your local pet store or favorite online retailer likely has extra-long leashes that you can use for recall training. Ask your helper to restrain your dog by holding onto his harness or with arms around his chest. Walk a short distance away and turn to face your puppy. Give the verbal command "come" and pat your knees or make kissing sounds. It's okay to use a lot of energy to get your puppy excited. Your excitement will encourage your puppy to come to you, rather than investigate the area around him.

As your handler releases your puppy, it can be helpful to take a few steps backward as your puppy approaches you. Encouraging him to chase you, if only for a few steps, gives him the feeling that this is a fun game, so he's more likely to repeat the behavior. Once he reaches you, reward him

Photo Courtesy of Alexys Berry

with plenty of praise and treats. Now that the dog is with you, it's your turn to hold him while your helper calls him over. You can repeat this process back and forth several times, but be sure to quit before your puppy gets tired or loses interest. With practice, you can increase the distance between you and your handler and ask your dog to come to you in increasingly distracting environments.

Off/Down

As the leader of your pack, you should be able to ask your dog to leave your favorite spot on the sofa. The "off" or "down" command will help you maintain order and respect. There can be some confusion between this command and the one used to ask your dog to lie down, so be sure to use different words. If you use "down" to ask your dog to lie down, you may want to use "off" to teach him to get off the furniture.

There are several methods that can be used to teach your dog to jump down off furniture. To use positive reinforcement, lure your dog with a treat while giving him the verbal command. Once all four paws hit the ground, you can reward him with the treat and plenty of praise. To combine this method with negative reinforcement, use gentle pressure on a leash to encourage your dog to jump down. If you've already taught your dog basic leash skills, this will be easy for him. You may also try gently pushing your dog toward the edge of the sofa with your hand, but use caution as some dogs respond badly to this type of pressure and may try to bite. You should also avoid grabbing your dog's collar with your hand to encourage him to jump down, as dogs with resource guarding or aggressive habits may bite. Using a leash will allow you to keep a safe distance in case your dog doesn't respond well to hand pressure.

Give/Drop

Puppies are notorious for chewing on inappropriate items, especially during teething, so it's essential that you teach your dog to give up whatever he has in his mouth. This command is also useful in preventing your dog from developing bad habits such as stealing items or resource guarding. If you plan on competing in dog sports, your dog may also be required to obey the give or drop command.

Rather than just pulling the object out of your dog's mouth, it's important that you teach him to give up the item willingly. Some dogs may respond to forceful removal with growling or even biting, so it's best to use positive reinforcement. The best way to get your dog to drop whatever he has is to make a trade. Just make sure that what you have is of higher value than

Photo Courtesy of
MaryAnn Hrobak

what he has. As you offer the treat, give your dog the verbal command and reward him once he lets go of the item. If your dog has resource guarding issues, you may want to try to lure him some distance away from the item with the treat before you take it away. If the item is something he's allowed to have, let him return to it after asking him to drop it. Once he's busy with the item again, repeat the process and ask him to drop it again. With practice, he'll readily drop whatever he has and come see what you have to offer instead.

Walk

Although Australian Cattle Dogs are not large, they are quite strong, so good leash manners are a must. Whether you plan on competing with your dog or just strolling around the neighborhood, he'll need to know how to walk politely on the leash without pulling you around. It should be noted that although there are many gimmicks available on the market to discourage pulling, the best way to discourage this bad habit is dedicated training. There is no quick fix, so be patient and consistent in your training.

To discourage pulling on the leash, it's important to only reward your dog when the leash is slack. Your puppy may believe that the leash means walking, so he'll get excited and try to pull you down the sidewalk. If he begins pulling, stop what you're doing and just stand there. He'll probably become confused and may even return to you to find out why you stopped.

Once there is slack in the lead, praise him and continue walking. If he begins pulling again, repeat the process. You may only be able to take a step or two at first, but with patience and practice, your dog will begin to understand what you're asking of him. If your dog is particularly energetic, it can be helpful to have a vigorous play session before practicing leash manners so that he's tired and less likely to try to drag you around. With practice, you can begin taking your dog more distracting environments to work on his leash manners.

Advanced Commands

Each of these basic commands can be used as the basis for more challenging commands, so don't be afraid to experiment with them. Try performing basic tasks in more distracting environments or increase the duration of certain commands. If you're in a safe environment, you can also try asking your dog to perform tasks off-leash or at a distance. You may also want to teach your dog tricks such as roll over, play dead, or sit pretty. If you're interested in competing in dog sports, try working with a trainer to teach your dog sport-specific commands. Australian Cattle Dogs are incredibly intelligent dogs, so the sky is the limit when it comes to what you can teach them.

Photo Courtesy of
Linda Multušová

CHAPTER 12
Training a Working Australian Cattle Dog

"Never start teaching them to work by themselves. Let them work with other dogs first. If you can't find any other working dogs (which sounds impossible to me) then you be the lead dog. You herd the livestock up front and keep them behind you. Start with one animal and one gate. 'Put 'em out!' and 'Put 'em up!' It is in their DNA."

James C Beel
ACD Breeder

The Importance of Basic Obedience

Before introducing your Australian Cattle Dog to livestock for the first time, it's essential that he have a basic understanding of obedience. Your dog should be able to focus on you and obey your commands before you take him into the distracting environment that he'll be working in as a cattle dog. He should come when he is called and be able to wait patiently at your side until he is needed. Without basic obedience, your dog may be able to move the livestock based on his instincts, but he will never be an effective working dog until he's able to incorporate your commands into his independent work.

Introducing Your Dog to Livestock

"Exposure to livestock and respect for livestock is essential as well as a good foundation of obedience training. Seek out a herding trainer that is familiar with this breed if you are not confident in training your own pup."

Gwen Shepperson
Buffalo Creek Cattle Dogs

Photo Courtesy of Lonnie Parsons

*Photo Courtesy of
Andrea Bennett*

The age at which many farmers or ranchers introduce their dogs to livestock varies, but it's generally recommended to avoid herding work until the dog is old enough to withstand the physical and mental rigors of the job. Of course, there's no harm in socializing him around certain animals. It's beneficial to introduce your dog to the sights and sounds of the farm or ranch at an early age, just don't expect him to move livestock until he's more mature.

If you have little to no experience with working dogs, you need to consult a professional working dog trainer as training a dog to safely herd livestock can be tricky. A responsible working dog handler cares not only about the safety and well-being of their dog, but about the livestock as well. Without proper instruction, your dog may become too aggressive. He could potentially chase the animals through a fence or get himself into a dangerous situation. An experienced trainer will be able to help you teach your dog how to move livestock as safely as possible.

The first time you introduce your Australian Cattle Dog to livestock, it may be best to keep him on a leash or long lead. This way, you'll be able to give him verbal commands to direct him, but you can still regain control if he chooses to ignore you. Even if your dog has a solid recall, he can easily become overwhelmed with the animals in front of him and ignore you. Keeping your dog on a long lead will enable you to intervene should he get too excited.

If you or the trainer you're working with has other working dogs available, it may be wise to let your dog work next to an experienced heeler for the first few sessions. The more experienced dog will provide your dog with a good example of what is expected of him. As pack animals, dogs will readily follow the lead of another, especially in situations where a more inexperienced dog may be unsure or anxious. You can still keep your dog on his long lead for a few sessions and when you begin to trust him more, let him off-leash to be guided by the more experienced dog.

If possible, you should only allow your dog to work with relatively calm livestock for the first few herding sessions. Allowing your dog to immediately interact with wild stock may overwhelm or frustrate him, possibly damaging his future as a working dog. Livestock that are used to being moved by dogs are more likely to do as they are asked, rather than become confrontational. Remember, in training you always want to set your dog up for success. As your dog gains experience, you'll be able to trust him to handle more challenging livestock, but for the first few weeks or months of his training, it's best to let him handle calmer animals. Soon, he'll have the confidence and skills to work even the wildest stock.

Herding-Specific Commands

"Your dog needs to know basic off leash commands fully before starting around stock; a biddable dog is half the battle, natural ability is the other. You need to be able to 'down' your dog and call him off stock before you can ensure the safety of the stock and dog while training. A properly trained working dog is worth more than a handful of hired ranch hands."

Kelsey Bolton
Flintlock Farms

Before you introduce your Australian Cattle Dog to livestock, it's a good idea to introduce herding-specific commands. Your dog's first herding session will be stressful enough, so you don't need to introduce new commands on top of an already overwhelming experience. Instead, get your dog used to listening to your commands and moving where you need him to go. In addition to a solid recall, your dog should be able to move in various directions as well as wait patiently until you give him further commands. It can be difficult to introduce certain commands without the context of livestock but do your best to get your dog used to the general idea of herding before he ever sets foot in the same field or pen as the cattle he'll be working.

Photo Courtesy of
Glenna Bochtler

Directional Commands

A significant aspect of herding livestock is positioning the dog so that the herd moves in the right direction. Since your dog won't know exactly where you need to move the herd, you'll need to teach him a few basic directional commands to help him understand where you need him to put pressure on the herd. Before introducing your dog to livestock, you can practice these commands on your daily walk or during a game of fetch or treibball.

The command "come-bye" or simply "bye" is used to tell your dog to move around the stock toward the left. By asking your dog to move in a clockwise direction around the herd, he'll be able to prevent the animals from moving toward the left or encourage them to move toward the right. If you notice any animals attempting to break out of the group, you'll be able to use this command to direct your dog toward the would-be escapees. Similarly, the command "away to me" or "away" will signal to your dog to move toward the right of the herd, in a counterclockwise direction.

If you find that your Australian Cattle Dog is putting too much pressure on the herd, or moving them too quickly, you'll need to direct him to move away from the stock. The command "get out" or "back" will instruct him to back off, but he'll understand that his work is not yet done. If the dog is working too closely to the herd, he may also be causing them unnecessary stress, so this command may also be used to prevent the stock from becoming too upset. It can also be used as a reprimand if the dog is becoming too aggressive in his work. To instruct your dog to move toward the stock, you'll need to teach him the command "walk up." Some handlers prefer "walk on" or simply "walk." If your dog is working the stock from a distance, this command will let him know that he needs to work more closely to the herd.

Wait

Occasionally, you may find that you need your dog to take a break from the livestock. The command "wait" is often used to let the dog know that he needs to stop what he's doing and wait for your next command.

You may have already taught him this command during his lessons in basic obedience, so he should understand this command well. Depending on your preference, you may ask your dog to wait while sitting, standing, or lying down. When teaching him this command, you can try asking your dog to wait in a variety of settings to encourage him to stop and focus on you, rather than what's happening around him.

Hold

The "hold" command is used to let your dog know that the herd is exactly where you need them to be and he needs to make sure they stay there. This command gives the dog free rein to do what is necessary to keep the herd in the specified location

Steady

If you find your dog is working the livestock too quickly, you can use the "steady" command to let him know that he needs to slow down. Working stock too quickly can result in breakaways or missed directions, so the steady command simply lets your dog know that he needs to slow down and focus on the job at hand.

Prior to working with livestock, you can teach your dog this command on your daily walks. As you give him the command, slow your pace. If he matches your pace, reward him with treats and praise. If he continues at the same pace, stop walking to return his focus to you. If you've done your homework with loose-leash walking, he should understand this concept fairly easily.

That'll Do

Once the livestock have been moved to where they need to go and the job is done, use the command "that'll do" to let your dog know that he's done. Most herding dogs are trained so that when they hear this command, they immediately leave the stock and return to their handler's side.

HELPFUL TIP
Cattle Dogs Love to Work

A Cattle Dog is never happier than when it's working. Giving your dog a job is the best way to keep her happy. That job doesn't need to be herding cattle or sheep. She could also be happy as a therapy dog or search and rescue dog.

You can teach your dog this command at home by using it to let him know when he's done playing or exploring the yard. Once your dog has had enough time outside, give him the command and encourage him to return to your side. You may need to combine this command with "come" until he understands what you're asking of him. Be sure to use plenty of praise to let him know he's done a good job.

Keeping Livestock Calm

In order for your dog to be an effective working dog, he must learn to work the herd in a way that puts as little stress on the animals as possible. It's important to keep the livestock calm because they are more likely to scatter or strike out if they become stressed or frightened. An overly excited dog can easily become too aggressive and scare the herd. If the animals scatter, especially if the terrain is difficult, it will be arduous and time-consuming to gather them up again. In most herding situations, time is of the essence, so you want your dog to learn to stay calm while he's working to prevent extra work for everyone.

As with any training situation, to encourage your dog to remain calm, you must display confident and quiet body language. If your dog senses that you are nervous or anxious, he may mirror that behavior or become protective. The livestock will also be more responsive if you approach them in a calm and collected manner. Although the group dynamics of prey animals are slightly different from those of predators, they'll recognize the body language of a leader and will be more likely to respond appropriately to you and your dog.

Problems You May Encounter While Working

"Do NOT allow your ACD to chase horses, if you are in an area where they will be exposed to them. This can get your dog seriously injured or killed, not to mention the damage that can be done to a horse's fragile tendons. These dogs are meant to drive cattle, which have MUCH thicker skin and stout legs, not horses."

Kelsey Bolton
Flintlock Farms

A common problem with inexperienced working dogs is too much grip, or aggression. If your dog runs into the herd and immediately latches onto a cow's nose, you must recognize his inappropriate behavior and correct it immediately. Regardless of whether your dog is working on a long lead or off-leash, call him back to you or ask him to back off. It's entirely possible that in his excited state of mind he may not listen to you, so you may need to pull him out of the herd with the leash. A dog that works with too much aggression isn't ready to be trusted off-leash yet, so take your time and

Photo Courtesy of
Karen Lotherington

go back to the basics. He likely just needs more experience to understand when that much pressure is necessary and when he needs to work with more subtle body language.

It's also possible for Australian Cattle Dogs to show fearful behavior around livestock. Animals such as cattle or horses can be quite large and intimidating so it's understandable that a dog may be nervous at first. Instead of continuing with herding training, you may need to back off and work on socializing your dog to livestock instead. You'll need to go back to the basics to teach him not to be afraid of the animals before you can let him practice his herding skills with confidence.

Although Australian Cattle Dogs have been bred for generations to work cattle, some dogs simply do not have any herding instinct. As the breed has risen in popularity, many individual dogs have been shown in conformation, agility, and obedience. Certain lines have been bred with a focus on conformation and athletic ability rather than instinct, so if a working dog is your goal, do your research and make sure your dog's pedigree is full of working cattle dogs rather than family pets. Unfortunately, it can be difficult or even impossible to get a dog interested in herding if he doesn't have the right instincts. If your dog seems uninterested in herding, you can try a few more training sessions to encourage him, but you may need to accept the fact that he's not interested. Forcing him to do work that he doesn't enjoy will be stressful and frustrating for you both.

CHAPTER 13
Unwanted Behaviors

What Is Bad Behavior in Dogs?

Unwanted behavior in dogs can range from relatively harmless actions, such as excessive barking, to life-threatening behaviors, such as running away. At the very least, bad behavior puts a serious strain on the relationships between your dog and the other members of your family. If left uncorrected, bad behaviors can escalate into more serious and difficult to solve problems.

Dogs do not develop serious behavioral problems overnight. It takes a consistent lack of correction over a lengthy period of time for dogs to develop a problem. Unfortunately, correcting bad behavior once it's begun is much more difficult and time consuming than preventing the behavior from developing in the first place, so if you see your dog behaving badly, the sooner you correct it the better.

Photo Courtesy of Kevin Black

Finding the Root of the Problem

"When trying to figure out if you and your family will be a good home for an ACD, remember they are a working dog. If they don't have a job, they will find one."

Kacy VanDuinen
Triple M Corgis (and Cattle Dogs)

The first step in correcting your Australian Cattle Dog's bad behavior is determining the cause. If you don't know what's causing the behavior, your corrections may improve your dog's behavior, but you'll never be able to completely solve the problem. For instance, if you know your dog barks excessively when he sees other dogs but not people, you'll know where to focus your training efforts. However, if all you know is that your dog barks too much, you're probably not going to be able to completely fix his behavior.

It's important to consider that the root of your dog's bad behavior may be your own behavior, so be prepared to reflect on your own actions. Australian Cattle Dogs are incredibly intuitive so your dog may be picking up on things you aren't aware that you're doing, such as holding his leash with tension. Your dog may be feeling your own anxiety or frustration and reacting accordingly. Remember, you must model ideal behavior for your dog whenever you enter a new situation. Be the calm, confident individual you want your dog to be.

Another likely cause of many problem behaviors is poor management of your dog's environment. You must always set your dog up for success in training; if you aren't managing his environment well, you're setting him up for failure. For instance, if you know your dog chews on the furniture when he isn't supervised, don't leave him unattended when he's out of his crate or designated area. By controlling your dog's environment, you can more accurately predict his actions and have better control over his behavior.

HELPFUL TIP
Avoid Boredom

Australian Cattle Dogs are extremely intelligent and have a ton of energy. Without at least two to three hours of vigorous exercise each day and plenty of mental stimulation, they can cause chaos. Many unwanted behaviors can be attributed to boredom, especially if those behaviors happen mostly when you aren't home. Try giving your Cattle Dog more exercise and leaving her with a puzzle toy or a frozen Kong toy filled with peanut butter to keep her busy.

Preventing Bad Behavior

It's much easier to prevent your dog from developing bad habits than it is to correct them. The key to bad behavior prevention is not allowing your dog to make the mistake in the first place. As previously mentioned, proper management of your dog's environment will help you to better control his behavior. An example of proper environmental management includes keeping trash cans out of your dog's reach. If you leave the trash out somewhere that your dog has access to, you're giving him the chance to develop a bad habit. The reward of delicious leftovers will serve as positive reinforcement for his actions, encouraging him to repeat the behavior in the future. However, if you don't give him the chance to get into the trash in the first place, he's less likely to learn bad behavior.

As with all aspects of dog training, consistency is key both in preventing and correcting bad behavior. If you are inconsistent in your expectations and actions, your dog is unlikely to learn the rules of house. If your dog gets away with bad behavior even occasionally, he's not going to learn what's right and wrong, he's just going to wonder why he only gets punished for certain behavior every once in a while.

Photo Courtesy of
Ross Terry

How to Properly Correct Your Australian Cattle Dog

When you correct your dog for bad behavior, it's important to adjust your level of correction to suit the behavior. For instance, you don't want to use a particularly harsh correction on your Australian Cattle Dog for barking at the neighbor, and you also don't want to use a simple "no" if he gets into a fight. No matter what bad behavior your dog exhibits, it's never appropriate to hit or kick your dog. Violent cor-

CAUTION

Not Good with Small Kids

Since Cattle Dogs are so prone to nipping, they don't make great additions to homes with small children, especially kids that like to run. Cattle Dogs mean no harm but are likely to bite children during play.

rections are unlikely to get you the results you're looking for and you'll only scare your dog. Depending on the dog, an aggressive correction may be met with an aggressive reaction and you may risk getting bitten. Even extreme behaviors can be corrected with a gentle touch and positive reinforcement.

Proper timing is essential when correcting your Australian Cattle Dog's bad behavior. If you come home to find that your dog has shredded the throw pillows, unfortunately, there's not much you can do except clean up the mess and move on. Dogs do not have the same understanding of the past that we do, and they will not understand the effects of things they've done earlier in the day. Therefore, if you punish your dog after the fact, he's not going to connect your corrections to what he did an hour ago, he's just going to become fearful. In order to properly correct your dog, you need to catch him in the act. If you come home and catch your dog with a mouth full of pillow stuffing, then you can correct the behavior knowing that he'll understand what he's done wrong.

Corrections can range from a firm "no" to loud claps and stomps. Anything that is loud and distracting, but not harmful, is a good correction. Other than a sharp "no," yelling should not be used as a correction except under extreme circumstances, such as a fight. Yelling will often frighten your dog and he may react badly. Some trainers also suggest using a spray bottle filled with clean water. Spritzing your dog in the face with water won't hurt him, but it will surprise him and discourage him from repeating the undesired behavior. If you have access to a hose or bucket of water in a serious situation such as a dog fight, using those is an appropriate response during an emergency.

Fixing Bad Habits

"Nipping at your heels or other people's heels should never be tolerated! This is unacceptable and means they need more vigorous training and correction, find another outlet for their desire to herd and gather. That may be through more exercise, proper correction and re-establishing a proper human/dog relationship."

Kelsey Bolton
Flintlock Farms

If you've been inconsistent in your training, you may find that your Australian Cattle Dog has developed some undesirable habits. Depending on the specific behavior that you're correcting, you may need to change your schedule or lifestyle to accommodate your dog's new training regimen. It's important to remember that everyone makes mistakes, so if your dog does develop a bad habit, it's not necessarily a negative reflection on you as an owner or trainer. Mistakes happen and you can use them as opportunities to learn and grow as a canine caretaker.

Photo Courtesy of Julie Timm

Regardless of whether you are working on the behavior alone or with a professional behaviorist or trainer, you need to understand that you're going to be working on your dog's behavior for a long time. Depending on the severity of the behavior, you may see very little improvement in the first few days, weeks, or even months. However, you must remain dedicated to your dog's training. It's easy to get frustrated, but keep your goals in mind and stay consistent in your training and you'll eventually begin to see improvements.

When to Call a Professional

There is no wrong time to consult with a professional behaviorist or dog trainer. Any time you think you could use a little guidance is the right time to call for help. It's better to seek guidance in the early stages, rather than allowing an issue to escalate into a more difficult problem. At the very least, bad manners can seriously damage the relationship between you and your Australian Cattle Dog. Professionals work with dogs of all sizes, breeds, and personalities, so no matter what you're dealing with, it's likely that the trainer has dealt with that problem before. He or she can help you to figure out the cause of the behavior and develop a training plan to fix the problem. The sooner you ask for help, the sooner you can find a solution.

If your dog is displaying aggressive, destructive, or fearful behavior, you need to consult a professional as soon as possible. Not only is extreme behavior difficult to manage, but it can quickly become dangerous. Professional behaviorists and trainers are experts in working with and managing aggressive or fearful dogs, so don't be afraid to seek help at the first sign.

Australian Cattle Dog–Specific Bad Habits

"ACD's can be aggressive. If caught young, you can correct it by not allowing it and by doing more socialization. Also, they are looking for a strong leader and, if they can't find it in you, they will become their own leader and that can lead to aggression."

Kacy VanDuinen
Triple M Corgis (and Cattle Dogs)

Australian Cattle Dogs were bred to herd cattle by nipping at their heels. Unfortunately, while this comes naturally to most Australian Cattle Dogs, they don't always only use this behavior on cattle. This behavior is especially common in families with small children. The dog may attempt to keep the kids under control by nipping at their heels or legs. Herding dogs may also try to herd other animals in the home, such as other dogs, which may result in a fight.

One of the best methods of discouraging your Australian Cattle Dog from nipping at people or animals is to imitate the sound that other dogs make when play becomes too rough. If your dog nips you, stop what you're doing and make a high-pitched yelping sound. Your dog will likely be star-tled and will stop what he's doing to figure out why you've made such a noise. While this may only momentarily distract him, with consistent repe-tition, he'll learn that nipping causes you to make an unpleasant sound and stops any game. Children are capable of performing this correction them-selves, but other animals may not be. Instead, you'll need to use a loud clap or stomp to distract your Australian Cattle Dog and discourage him from trying to herd other pets.

Australian Cattle Dogs are intelligent, high-energy dogs and need plen-ty of mental and physical stimulation in order to prevent boredom. Dogs that do not receive enough exercise may become destructive and you may

Photo Courtesy of Carrie Jurkiewicz

find them chewing up furniture or shoes or digging in the yard. Remember, a tired dog is a well-behaved dog, so if your Australian Cattle Dog begins to exhibit destructive behavior, he may simply need more stimulation throughout the day.

Due to the naturally suspicious nature of the breed, some Australian Cattle Dogs can become aggressive with strangers if not properly socialized. Some dogs may never approach a stranger with a wagging tail and friendly demeanor, but they can be taught to tolerate new people without reacting aggressively. Introduce your dog to as many different types of people as you can and always reward appropriate behavior. If your Australian Cattle Dog displays inappropriate behavior such as growling, barking, or avoidance, be sure to correct such behavior. Remember, a treat from a friendly stranger can be a big help in convincing your dog that new people are not to be feared.

CHAPTER 14
Traveling with Australian Cattle Dogs

"ACDs love to go with their owner as much as possible! Just make certain they have ample time to exercise after long trips."

Gwen Shepperson
Buffalo Creek Cattle Dogs

Dog Carriers and Car Restraints

When traveling with your Australian Cattle Dog by car, you have several options to keep him safe and restrained during your trip. It's important to be aware that certain restraints may not fit as well in certain cars, so you may need to verify that your chosen option will work in your particular model of car. Likewise, some dogs may prefer one type of restraint over another, so don't be afraid to try out a few options to see what works best. As your Australian Cattle Dog gains more experience trav-

Photo Courtesy of
Jesse du Pree

eling, he may become more comfortable with travel and you can then adjust his restraint as needed.

One of the most popular options for restraining dogs in cars is a crate or carrier. Crates can be made from a variety of materials including metal, plastic, and mesh fabric. Most carriers are available in a variety of sizes to suit Australian Cattle Dogs of all ages and sizes. Plastic or metal wire crates will usually be the cheapest and most versatile choice, so if you're on a budget or think you'll need to change sizes as your puppy grows, these may be your best option. Soft-sided fabric crates are easy to transport, but are not as durable, especially if your dog is a chewer. There are a few companies that manufacture heavy-duty metal crates that have been crash tested for safety, but they can be rather expensive. No matter what type of crate you choose, make sure it's large enough for your dog to comfortably stand up, lie down, and turn around.

If you would prefer to give your Australian Cattle Dog a bit more freedom than a crate, or your car won't comfortably fit an appropriately sized crate, consider using a barrier to keep your dog safely restrained in the back seat or cargo area. Most barriers are made of either metal or mesh cloth and are either pressure mounted or attach to the seats' headrests with straps. Barriers come in a variety of sizes so you should be able to find one that fits your specific vehicle. You may need to consider other options if your dog has a tendency to bolt out the car door as soon as you open it. Barriers only keep your dog from jumping into the front seat, so you'll still need to be careful opening the car doors to let him out.

Doggy seat belts are becoming increasingly popular with dog owners and are a great option for safe car travel. Most seat belts for dogs consist of a short leash with a seatbelt latch plate on one end that can be clipped into your vehicle's seatbelt buckle. The other end of the leash can then be attached to a harness. Harnesses are generally recommended over collars because your dog could become seriously injured in a crash if he's only restrained by his neck. Harnesses spread the pressure out across the dog's chest and torso, decreasing the likelihood of serious injury.

Regardless of the type of restraint you choose, be sure to keep your dog safely restrained every time he travels with you, even if it's just across town. A loose dog in the car is a danger to you as well as the other drivers on the road. Your dog could easily jump into your lap while you're driving and cause a wreck. Should you have an accident, an unrestrained dog is more likely to become injured in the crash and may be able to escape the car and run away or be further injured by surrounding traffic. Just like with your human family members, you must always enforce proper safety rules while in the car with your dog.

Preparing Your Australian Cattle Dog for Car Rides

Before you take your new Australian Cattle Dog on his first road trip, you need to consider how prepared he is to travel. If he's an experienced traveler, you'll be able to pack up and go with minimal trouble. However, if he hasn't traveled much before, you may need to be more cautious. Limiting your dog's food and water before traveling can help limit carsickness. Some dogs can handle small amounts of food or water, but if your dog doesn't travel well on a full stomach, you may just have to wait to feed him until you reach your destination. Bring along a few towels or extra blankets to help with cleanup if your dog does get carsick. A waterproof seat protector is a great investment if your dog is traveling in the back seat with a barrier or seatbelt. Kennels or carriers are the easiest to clean, so if you know your dog gets carsick, you may want to have him travel in a crate. Lining the crate with disposable puppy pads can also help you clean up with ease.

Remember to give your dog regular bathroom breaks during your travels. Depending on the age of your dog, you may need to stop every few hours so he can relieve himself. If you already have a potty break schedule at home, try sticking to that while you travel. Consistency is key in housetraining, even when you're on the road.

Photo Courtesy of Theresa Amaro

Before you leave home, double check to make sure crates, barriers, or seatbelts are in working order. You should also make sure you have everything your dog will need while you're away. If you'll be gone for several days or longer, make sure that you have enough food for the duration of your trip. You'll also want to make sure you have all leashes, collars, bowls, and waste bags. Checking before you leave will prevent you from panicking when you reach your destination only to realize you left your dog's food sitting on the kitchen counter.

Photo Courtesy of
Leanne Darrell

Flying and Hotel Stays

If you plan on flying to your destination or staying in a hotel when you get there, it's best to make arrangements as far in advance as possible. Be sure that the airline or hotel you're using allows dogs so you don't arrive at the airport or hotel only to find that your dog won't be permitted to join you. Remember, it's common for both airlines and hotels to charge extra fees for dogs, so be sure to budget accordingly. Fees will vary by company, so be sure to ask when you're booking your ticket or room.

Unless you're traveling with a young puppy, most airlines will consider Australian Cattle Dogs too large to travel with you in the cabin. So if you plan on flying with your dog, he will likely be traveling in the cargo area of the plane. Although this may sound like an unpleasant experience, most planes have areas in their cargo space specifically designated for pets. These areas are climate controlled and often lighted to keep animals comfortable. All kennels are secured before takeoff to prevent them from shifting, rolling, or falling.

Before flying with your Australian Cattle Dog, you need to make sure that the crate your dog will be traveling in is airline approved. Requirements vary by airline, so be sure to check with an airline representative before you arrive at the airport. All crates are required to be properly labeled, ventilated, and secure. As with any crate, it should be large enough for your dog to lie down, stand up, and turn around comfortably.

Photo Courtesy of
Amanda Willman

In the months or weeks before your trip, you should allow your dog to become comfortable in the crate that he'll be traveling in. Shoving him into an unfamiliar crate minutes before you leave for the airport is a recipe for disaster. As with regular crate training, you want your dog to understand that the crate is a source of comfort and security rather than stress. Try placing blankets or towels that your dog is familiar with in the crate, especially on the day you'll be traveling. Having the familiar scent of home in a comfortable crate will help reduce your dog's stress and anxiety.

HELPFUL TIP
Exercise Before Traveling

Since Australian Cattle Dogs have so much energy, they can get antsy during travel. Plan ahead and take your dog for a very long hike or a day at doggy day care the day before a big trip to help her stay calm.

Dog-friendly hotels can be found across the country, but they vary in the services they offer. Some hotels may simply tolerate dogs, while others may offer off-leash areas, beds, bowls, and more. No matter how dog-friendly a hotel is, it's important for your dog to be on his best behavior while staying there. Bringing an out-of-control, barking Australian Cattle Dog into a hotel will not leave a positive impression on either the staff or the other guests and you may even be asked to leave or to pay additional fees. Proper training and socialization are essential in teaching your dog to be a respectful guest of any establishment.

Kenneling vs. Dog Sitters

Unfortunately, it's not always possible to take your Australian Cattle Dog with you when you travel. When those situations arise, you'll need to find a trusted facility or individual to care for your beloved dog while you're away. You should never just leave your dog with the first sitter or facility that you find. Instead, do thorough research to find the right fit for your budget and your dog.

Depending on the area you live in, you may have quite a few boarding facilities to choose from. Boarding can vary widely in cost based on the quality of care and services provided. Basic boarding kennels usually keep your dog in a relatively simple cage or run and allow him time outside two or three times a day. If you have multiple dogs, they may be allowed to share one kennel if it's big enough. These types of facilities are not usually staffed overnight. Higher-end boarding facilities will offer more comfort

141

Photo Courtesy of
Ginger Nowak

for your dog, but at a bigger price. Some facilities offer kennels with elevated beds, televisions, and different exercise options. You can often choose to have your dog walked on a leash or sign him up for individual or group play sessions. For social dogs, playgroups can be an ideal way to keep your dog exercised and stimulated. For shy dogs or those not fond of big groups, individual play sessions are a great way to make sure your dog receives the attention and exercise he craves while you're away. One of the newest trends in boarding is cage-free facilities. Dogs are supervised 24/7 so they can eat, sleep, and play as a group, without ever having to spend time in a kennel.

If the idea of a busy boarding facility seems too stressful for your dog, you may want to search for a dog sitter. Some areas have pet sitting companies which send employees out to your home to take care of your pets, but you can also find individuals willing to care for your dog while you're away. Self-employed sitters may be willing to keep your dog in their own homes, so he's never alone. Having a sitter stay at your house is an excellent option for dogs who are nervous in new environments. Most sitters are also willing to water your plants, collect your newspapers or mail, and keep your home secure. Pet sitters are usually more expensive than boarding facilities, simply because of the level of care they offer.

Whether you choose to leave your precious pooch in the caring hands of a boarding facility staff or a pet sitter, you'll need to make sure your dog is comfortable before you leave. Many facilities and sitters offer a trial run, where you can leave your Australian Cattle Dog for the day to make sure it's a good fit. Knowing your dog is happy and comfortable will allow you to travel without having to worry about his well-being.

If you're having a sitter come to your home, you'll need to make sure you have enough dog food to last for the duration of your trip. You'll also need to make sure the sitter knows where your dog's supplies are located

Photo Courtesy of
Melissa Lynch

to make sure he or she has everything they need to care for your dog. You should also let the sitter know how to reach you while you're away and provide your dog's veterinarian's contact information. Most boarding facilities will also ask for this information in case of an emergency. If you're boarding your dog, you'll also want to make sure to leave the staff with a list of your dog's belongings to make sure everything gets returned to you when you pick your dog up. Labeling everything with your dog's name or your last name can also be helpful. Regardless of whether your dog is traveling with you or staying at a boarding kennel, preparation is key to a successful and stress-free trip.

CHAPTER 15
Nutrition

Importance of Good Diet

"ACD's are prone to Pancreatitis, or bloody butt. Keep them on a regular diet of premium dog food and stay with that. Any changes in diet may, or may not, cause your new puppy to have blood in their stools and leaking from behind."

James C Beel
ACD Breeder

One of the most important aspects of keeping your Australian Cattle Dog healthy is a well-balanced diet. A healthy diet is especially important for growing puppies, who must receive the correct vitamins and minerals to

Photo Courtesy of
Whitney Doherty

grow strong bones and healthy muscles. The fats and proteins in a good diet help keep your dog's body in good shape, giving him the energy to herd cattle, compete in the show ring, or accompany you on a hike.

Without a healthy diet, a dog can develop serious health conditions such as pancreatitis, heart disease, and bladder or kidney stones. However, the most common diet-related problem facing dogs is obesity. While it's important to provide your dog with good nutrition, you must also complement his diet with proper portion sizes and adequate exercise in order to keep him at a healthy weight.

> **HELPFUL TIP**
> **The Importance of a Good Diet**
>
> Even dog foods that claim to be nutritionally complete can be bad for your dog. Some commercial dog foods are the canine equivalent of fast food—they taste good, but they aren't good for you.
> Your dog's food should have real meat as the first ingredient. Avoid meat by-products, corn, artificial flavors, colors, or preservatives. The higher the quality of food you feed your dog, the healthier she will be.

In order to ensure that pets receive the nutrients they need to thrive, commercial pet foods are held to certain standards and can be recalled if they do not meet those standards. These standards are government regulated, so you can be sure that the food you buy at your local pet store has been evaluated and determined to provide your dog with everything he needs to life a long and healthy life.

You may also choose to feed your dog a homemade diet, but it's important to understand that you are then responsible for ensuring that your dog's diet is nutritionally sound. If you are interested in making your dog's food at home, you should consult a veterinary nutritionist to make sure that your dog's homemade diet is providing him with essential nutrients.

The number of choices you have when deciding what to feed your dog can be overwhelming, but it's important to remember that there is no single perfect dog food. What you feed your dog will depend on his age, health, and activity level as well as your budget for both time and money. If your Australian Cattle Dog is a picky eater, you may need to try a few different foods to find one he likes, so don't be afraid to experiment. If you have any questions about your dog's diet, be sure to discuss it with your veterinarian at your dog's next checkup.

Different Types of Commercial Food

Kibble is by far the most popular type of commercial dog food available. The crunchy brown nuggets are likely what you picture when you think of dog food. Kibble's popularity is due to both its convenience and its incredible variety. Kibble also varies in cost, making it appropriate for owners on a budget as well as those looking to spoil their dogs. Most brands of kibble offer puppy, adult, and senior recipes to suit dogs of all ages. Some companies have even developed kibble appropriate for all life stages, eliminating the need to switch foods when your dog reaches a certain age. If your dog has any food sensitivities or dietary restrictions, you'll be able to find a kibble to suit his needs. Kibble made with limited ingredients or uncommon proteins, such as whitefish or kangaroo, is ideal for dogs with food al-

Photo Courtesy of
Andrea Bennett

lergies. Grain-free is also a popular choice for owners looking to feed their dogs a more protein-focused diet. If your dog has a medical condition, such as heart disease or even arthritis, you can find a food to help ease his symptoms. Some kibble is available by prescription only, so if your dog needs a specific type of food due to his health, you'll need to get it from your vet. Kibble is the ideal food for dogs with busy families. You can simply measure out your dog's daily portion and pour it into his bowl at mealtime. An added benefit of kibble is that the crunchy texture can help scrape tartar off your dog's teeth.

Canned food is a close second in terms of popularity. Much like kibble, canned food is available in an incredible number of formulas and varieties to suit dogs of all sizes, ages, and needs. Many types of prescription kibble also have a canned version for dogs who prefer wet food. Canned food is a great choice for picky eaters, as they usually find it more appealing than dry kibble. It's also ideal for dogs with dental problems since it requires relatively little chewing. However, the soft and sticky nature of canned food can contribute to dental disease, so if you choose to feed it to your dog, be sure to offer him chew toys, brush his teeth, or have your veterinarian perform regular teeth cleanings.

One of the newest types of food available on the pet food market can be found in your local pet store's refrigerated section. Fresh, refrigerated dog food is typically packaged into tubes, which can be sliced to your preferred portion size and then covered and placed back into the refrigerator. Like canned food, many dogs find refrigerated food to be more palatable than kibble, but it lacks the teeth cleaning qualities of crunchier food.

More dog owners are choosing to feed their dogs like their wild ancestors, leading to the development of commercial raw dog food, now found in your local pet store's freezer section. Commercial raw food is the easiest way to provide your dog with a raw diet without the hassle of preparing it yourself. You also don't need to worry about making sure your dog's meals are properly balanced as commercial raw food must meet specific nutritional standards. Depending on the size of your dog, you can find raw food in kibble-sized pieces, larger nuggets, or even patties. The smaller pieces can simply be scooped out with a measuring cup and fed once thawed. The nuggets and patties are ideal for larger dogs and can be placed directly into your dog's bowl to thaw or cut in half if your dog needs a smaller portion.

Homemade Foods and Recipes

If you plan on making your dog's food, you need to make sure you are feeding a nutritionally balanced diet. Dietary deficiencies typically take a long time to show up and by that time the damage may have already been done. If you have any doubts about homemade diets, it's best to consult with a canine nutritionist who can help you develop a healthy and balanced diet for your Australian Cattle Dog.

Raw diets are typically divided into two categories. The first category is referred to as Prey Model Raw, or PMR, and is meant to imitate a wild dog's natural diet in terms of prey. PMR diets typically consist of 80% muscle meat, 10% bone, and 10% organ. Some vegetables and fruits can be added in small quantities. Most PMR diets do not include vegetables. The second category of raw diets is called Biologically Appropriate Raw Food, or BARF. It's quite similar to PMR, but allows for the addition of vegetables, fruits, and even some grains. Many raw feeders choose to supplement their dogs' diets with additions such as goat's milk or fish oil to help make up for any nutritional deficiencies. Variety is essential in homemade raw diets as different types of protein contain different nutrients. As with any homemade diet, one of the downsides of a raw diet is the time it takes to prepare your dog's meals. Many raw feeders dedicated several hours per week to preparing and balancing their dogs' diets.

Photo Courtesy of Tiffany Hughes

Cooked diets, typically consisting of meat, organs, eggs, vegetables, and grains, are another option for those who wish to feed their dogs homemade food. As with raw diets, balance and variety is essential. Cooked diets are a great option for picky dogs, especially those that turn up

*Photo Courtesy of
Kylee Bouchard*

their nose at raw food. Although cooking does remove some of the nutrients in ingredients, variety and supplements can easily make up for any nutrient loss due to cooking temperature. Unlike raw diets, which offer raw bones that aid in teeth cleaning, dogs who eat a cooked diet may face the same dental problems as those fed canned or refrigerated commercial food, so it's important to monitor your dog's dental health. Cooked diets can also be quite time consuming, so if you don't have much spare time to spend cooking your dog's meals each week, you may want to consider a commercial diet.

People Food—Harmful and Acceptable Kinds

If you insist on feeding your Australian Cattle Dog human food, it's best to stick with foods that are healthy. Most vegetables are harmless for dogs if fed in moderation. Many dogs enjoy veggies such as carrots, peas, zucchini, and beets. Leafy greens such as spinach, kale, or collard greens are also fine. Many types of fruit are also safe to feed your dog, but since fruit can be high in sugar, it's best to use it only as an occasional treat. Non-toxic fruits include blueberries, raspberries, apples, and bananas. Cantaloupe, watermelon, and cranberries are also safe for dogs. Not all fruits and vegetables are safe to feed dogs, however, so avoid giving your dog onions, grapes, and garlic. Fruits with pits can also be harmful for dogs, so it's best to avoid them.

Some types of people food are okay for your dog to eat in small amounts. Cheese and peanut butter are popular treats for dogs but are quite high in fat. Those extra calories not only add inches to your dog's waistline, but the high fat content puts unnecessary extra strain on your dog's vital organs. Rather than risk your dog's health, it's best to limit or avoid high-fat people food.

Most dog owners are aware of common foods that are toxic to dogs, such as chocolate and alcohol, but there are a few other human foods that can be harmful if consumed by your dog. Sugar-free foods that contain the ingredient xylitol can be incredibly poisonous to dogs. Foods or drinks containing caffeine can also put your dog's life at risk. If you suspect your dog has consumed any toxic food, take him to your veterinarian immediately. The sooner you seek treatment, the more likely your dog is to survive. If you're wondering if a food is safe for your dog to consume, the American Kennel Club has a comprehensive list of safe and toxic human foods on their website.

Weight Management

"Typically Cattle dogs are easy keepers, meaning they don't usually suffer from health issues or skin problems requiring special diets. They will quickly and easily become over weight if they are fed too rich a diet, so watching their weight is important."

Kelsey Bolton
Flintlock Farms

Over half of all adult dogs in the United States are considered overweight or obese. Excess weight can be detrimental to your dog's health so proper weight management is essential. Even a few extra pounds can put extra strain on your dog's joints, leading to arthritis and potential injury. This can limit a dog's mobility, leading to even more weight gain if his diet doesn't change according to his activity level. Obesity can also contribute to heart disease and diabetes. To help your dog life a long and happy life, make sure you keep track of your dog's diet and exercise and consult your veterinarian if you have any questions.

Most types of commercial food have suggested portion sizes listed on their packaging, but it's important to understand that those are just suggestions. Your dog's portion size should be adjusted according to his age and activity level. Active, growing puppies obviously need more calories than sedentary older dogs. The best way to determine your Australian Cattle Dog's ideal portion size is to keep an eye on his weight. If you notice any weight gain or loss, adjust

Photo Courtesy of Samantha Runyon

his meal size accordingly. Remember to include training treats and snacks when calculating portion sizes, not just meals.

Many dogs will finish a meal and then beg for more and it can be tempting to give in. However, you are responsible for keeping your dog as healthy as possible, so you must resist when your dog asks for more. If you just can't say no, consider feeding your dog low-calorie snacks such as vegetables. You can also find low-calorie dog food, which contains more fillers and fewer calories than regular food. The best way to allow your dog to have more food is to keep him active. The more active your dog is, the more he can eat. More activity will also keep him physically and mentally fit.

CHAPTER 16
Grooming Your Australian Cattle Dog

Coat Basics

"They are considered a wash and wear breed, very low maintenance coats and require little grooming. They are a double coated breed, meaning they have a plush layer of fur underneath a top coat of more coarse protective guard hairs."

Kelsey Bolton
Flintlock Farms

Australian Cattle Dogs require very little care in terms of grooming. The breed was created to work in rugged conditions, so their coat is meant to be as low maintenance as possible. Australian Cattle Dogs have double coats, which means they have two types of hair. The undercoat is soft, fine, and grows close to the skin. It's meant to insulate the dog against both heat and cold. The second type of hair is called guard hairs, which make up the outer layer of the coat and seal in your dog's natural body temperature, protecting him from dirt and water. Together, the two types of hair create a coat that is water-resistant, insulating, and protective. A double-coated dog will only need the occasional bath and brushing and should never be cut or shaved. Shaving a double-coated dog can result in permanent damage to the coat and it may never grow back quite the same.

Australian Cattle Dogs are considered moderate shedders for most of the year. Typically, they shed heavily twice per year, in the spring and fall. Regular brushing can help limit the amount of dog hair your dog leaves around your house and on your furniture. Certain shampoos and conditioners are also designed to help remove your dog's dead coat and limit his shedding between grooming sessions. If you're struggling with your dog's seasonal shedding, don't be afraid to consult your local groomer. They're experts in deshedding and can help you find the right products to help you keep your dog's coat healthy.

Bathing and Brushing

"ACD's shed profusely! You can generally expect heavy seasonal shedding in spring and fall as well as general shedding the rest of the year."

Alison Whittington
Hardtack Australian Cattle Dogs

Australian Cattle Dogs' coats are easy to care for, so you likely won't need to bathe your new dog very frequently. Many owners choose to only bathe their dogs when they get especially dirty, such as after playing the mud or rolling in something smelly. Bathing should be done frequently enough that any dead hair and skin, dirt, and excess oil can be removed before it causes problems. However, bathing too frequently can strip the coat

Photo Courtesy of
Bonnie Pastino

Photo Courtesy of Karacel Hayman

of its natural oils and cause dryness and itching. A bath every 4-8 weeks should be enough to keep your dog looking and smelling great. If you're unsure about how often you should bathe your dog, consult your local groomer. He or she will be able to examine your dog's coat and lifestyle and make the appropriate recommendation.

The type of shampoo and conditioner you use will largely depend on the condition of your dog's coat and skin, as well as your own preferences. If your Australian Cattle Dog suffers from allergies, a soothing oatmeal shampoo can help ease his itchiness. There are shampoos to suit every need from being sprayed by a skunk to flea control, so it's up to you to choose an appropriate product. If you or your dog are sensitive to strong smells, you can even find mild shampoos that will clean your dog without leaving an overpowering scent. Be sure to look at the ingredients before purchasing a shampoo or conditioner. Natural products are less likely to irritate your dog's skin or cause a reaction, so try to choose a product that contains fewer artificial ingredients or chemicals.

When bathing your Australian Cattle Dog, it's best to thoroughly wet the coat before applying shampoo. Try to avoid getting water in your dog's ears, eyes, and nose. You can either apply the shampoo with your hands or with a grooming tool, such as a rubber curry brush or grooming glove. While scrubbing your dog, be sure to get the shampoo through the coat and down to the skin. Otherwise, you're only washing to top part of the coat without removing the dead hair, skin, and dirt near the skin's surface. Scrub every inch of your dog, using caution around delicate body parts such as the face and legs. Avoid getting shampoo in your dog's ears and eyes, as this can cause serious irritation or even permanent damage. It can be helpful to place cotton balls in your dog's ears prior to the bath but be sure to remove them when you're done. Once you're sure you've thoroughly shampooed him, it's time to rinse your dog. It's important to remove all shampoo from the coat to prevent irritation. Most professional groomers recommend rinsing until you're certain the shampoo is gone, then rinsing one more time just to be sure. Conditioner is not necessary, but it can be helpful for itchy skin or dry coats, so if you use conditioner just repeat these steps and be sure to rinse all conditioner from the coat afterwards.

Australian Cattle Dogs require little brushing as their coats do not matt or tangle. However, brushing is beneficial to the health of your dog's skin and coat. Not only does it feel good, but it helps distribute the coat's natural oils, stimulate blood flow in the skin, and remove dead hair. Regular brushing can also help with seasonal shedding as it reduces the amount of hair left around your house. It's not necessary to brush your dog every day unless it's something you both enjoy. Two or three brushing sessions per week should be plenty to keep your dog looking and feeling great.

One of the best grooming tools to use on an Australian Cattle Dog is a rubber curry brush. The rubber brush can be used wet or dry to remove dead hair and skin cells. To use, simply massage your dog in circular motion over his body. Use gentle pressure and avoid delicate areas such as the face and legs. Grooming gloves can be another useful tool for keeping your dog's coat in good health. The gloves simply slip over your hand and feature small rubber or plastic nubs across the palm and fingers. They can be used in the same way as the rubber curry brush. Shedding blades, such

HELPFUL TIP
Prepare for Shedding

Australian Cattle Dogs shed a lot. The best way to reduce shedding is to use a rubber curry-style brush daily and a deshedding tool (like a FURminator) once a week. A poor diet can cause excess shedding, so feed your Cattle Dog a high-quality diet.

as the Furminator, are another option, but they must be used carefully to avoid damaging the skin and coat. Use only gentle pressure and do not overbrush or apply hard pressure which can break hairs and scrape skin. If you're unsure about what tool is best to use for grooming your dog, your local groomer will be able to make a recommendation based on your dog's coat condition and your preferences.

Trimming the Nails

Long nails can put uncomfortable pressure on your dog's toes and can even affect how he walks, so nails should be trimmed at least every four to six weeks to keep them in good condition.

There are two methods that can be used to trim your Australian Cattle Dog's nails. The most popular method is the use of traditional scissor-type nail trimmers. Scissor-type trimmers are usually recommended over guillotine-type trimmers as the latter tends to crush the nail, rather than cut cleanly. The second method is becoming more popular as dog owners recognize the benefits of grinding the nails. Dremel-style tools are used to grind the sharp points off the nail, creating a rounded nail tip. The benefit

Photo Courtesy of Max Wood

Photo Courtesy of
Bonnie Pastino

of grinding over trimming is that there are no sharp edges to scratch you or your furniture. Although the sound of the grinder can take time for your dog to get used to, most dogs prefer grinders over trimmers.

Trimming your Australian Cattle Dog's nails at home is a relatively easy process. First, hold your dog's paw and examine his nails, looking for the quick. If your dog has black nails, you may not be able to see the quick and will have to guess, but with white nails you'll be able to see approximately how much you can cut off. When you begin to trim or grind your dog's nails, take only a small layer off at a time. This will help prevent you from cutting the quick. As you cut, a small, dark circle will eventually appear in the nail. This is the tip of the quick and you should stop trimming. If you do accidentally cut the quick, styptic powder or gel is a great way to rapidly stop the bleeding.

If you'd rather not trim your dog's nails yourself, your local veterinarian or groomer will be able to do it for a relatively low price. Nail trimming is inexpensive and can typically be done without an appointment, but it's best to call to make sure. Veterinary teams and groomers are experts in teaching dogs to stand quietly for nail trimming, so if you're struggling to get the job done at home, you may want to reach out to a professional for assistance.

Brushing Their Teeth

Brushing your Australian Cattle Dog's teeth is a great way to prevent dental disease and reduce the frequency of professional dental cleanings. However, brushing is only effective if it's done every day. As you can imagine with your own teeth, if you were to brush only occasionally, instead of daily, you'd likely begin to see plaque and tartar buildup rather quickly. It can be difficult to get started with this daily routine, but with practice you'll be able to brush your dog's teeth with ease. Taking a few minutes out of your day to take care of your dog's teeth is a small sacrifice when it comes to his health.

Doggy toothbrushes typically come in two different types. The first resembles your own toothbrush, with a long handle and bristles at one end. The other is typically made of silicon or rubber and slips over your finger. The end of the finger brush is covered in small bristles. Finger brushes should only be used on dogs that can be trusted not to bite down. Human toothpastes contain ingredients that can be harmful to dogs, so only use doggy toothpastes, which are designed to be swallowed in small amounts so they are completely safe. They are available in a wide variety of flavors from vanilla and peanut butter to chicken and beef, so choose one that will appeal to your dog.

To start brushing your dog's teeth, try putting a small amount of toothpaste on the brush and letting your Australian Cattle Dog lick it off. As he gets used to the brush and the flavor of the toothpaste you can begin brushing. At first, you may only be able to brush for a second or two, but with practice you'll be able to brush all of your dog's teeth. Go slowly and try not to rush the process. Be sure to use plenty of praise when your dog stands quietly.

Cleaning Ears and Eyes

Since Australian Cattle Dogs have upright ears with plenty of airflow, ear infections are less common than in drop eared breeds. However, you may need to clean your dog's ears out occasionally to prevent a buildup of dirt and wax. Cleaning should also be done after bathing or swimming to help remove excess water. Cleaning your dog's eyes should be done anytime you notice a buildup of discharge or dirt.

Your local pet store or favorite online retailer likely has quite a few ear cleaners to choose from. Some ear cleaners are alcohol-based, and you want to avoid these if your dog has sensitive ears. Alcohol can cause an unpleasant burning sensation on sore or irritated ears. However, if your dog has perfectly healthy ears, alcohol can help dry out a wet ear, so it may be appropriate to use after swimming or bathing. Non-alcohol-based cleaners work just as well, so it's up to you to decide what's best for your dog.

To clean your dog's ears, soak a cotton ball in the ear cleaner of your choice. Cotton balls should always be used over cotton swabs. Your fingers and a cotton ball are too large to reach any of the delicate structures of the ear so you can rest assured that you can't hurt your dog. Cotton swabs, on the other hand, can reach far into the ear and can cause damage if inserted too far or if your dog shakes his head. Once you've soaked the cotton ball, use it to wipe around your dog's ear canal and as far in as you can reach. Use gentle pressure to clean so that you don't hurt your dog. After you remove as much residue as possible, you can use a dry cotton ball to wipe up any excess cleaner.

Eye cleaner is generally available in a bottle or in pre-soaked pads. The bottle is convenient if you'd prefer to use cotton balls or a soft cloth to clean your dog's eyes, but the pre-soaked pads are often more convenient. To use, wet your cloth or cotton ball, or use a pre-soaked pad, and gently wipe around your dog's eye area. Use gentle pressure to remove any discharge. If the discharge has become dry and crusty, you may need to wipe a few times to completely remove it. As always, be sure to praise your Australian Cattle Dog for being patient during this process.

When Professional Help Is Necessary

Don't be afraid to seek professional grooming help at any time. You don't need to be struggling with the grooming process to contact a professional. There's no shame in having someone else to the dirty work for you. Groomers are experts in coat and skin care and can help you take the best care possible of your dog. They'll be able to look over every inch of your dog to make sure he's healthy. In addition to bathing and brushing, groomers will trim your dog's nails, clean his ears and eyes, and may even brush his teeth if you ask. They're also experts in dealing with difficult or impatient dogs, so if your dog is becoming difficult to groom, a patient and understanding groomer will be able to teach him to stand nicely while he's being groomed.

CHAPTER 17
Basic Health Care

Visiting the Vet

Regular veterinary appointments are crucial in keeping your Australian Cattle Dog healthy. Most vets recommend a basic examination every six to twelve months, depending on your dog's age and health. If your dog is in good health, you may feel that it's unnecessary to take your dog to the vet that often, but frequent visits will ensure that any health problems are detected and treated before they become a serious problem. Regular vaccinations and deworming will also help protect your dog from parasites and disease. It will also give you the opportunity to discuss your dog's diet and weight with your vet and allow him or her the opportunity to recommend any changes to your dog's lifestyle.

Photo Courtesy of Kelsey Harville

Fleas and Ticks

Preventing external parasites is essential, not only for the sake of your Australian Cattle Dog, but for your entire family. Fleas and ticks are capable of carrying and transmitting a number of diseases. If these parasites are brought into your home by your dog, your human family members are also at risk of being bitten and infected. Fleas are known to carry tapeworms, which can then be passed onto your dog when he accidentally ingests a tapeworm-infested flea while chewing at his itchy skin. This itchiness, known as flea allergy dermatitis, is a common reaction and is caused by your dog's immune system reacting to the fleas' saliva. Fleas also carry bartonellosis, which can be passed to humans, and can cause severe anemia. Ticks are also responsible for transmitting disease to both dogs and humans. Lyme disease, Rocky Mountain spotted fever, babesiosis, and ehrlichiosis are all carried by different species of ticks depending on the area you live in. To keep your family and pets safe from disease, flea and tick prevention is crucial.

HELPFUL TIP
Health Conditions

While Australian Cattle Dogs are generally healthy, they are prone to hip dysplasia, deafness, and progressive retinal atrophy (a condition that causes blindness). Make sure to get your Cattle Dog puppy from a reputable breeder who does health testing on the parent dogs.

In some areas, year-round flea and tick prevention may not be necessary, but you should check with your veterinarian to determine how frequently you need to administer flea and tick prevention medication. If you frequently board your dog or take him to daycare, you may need to treat your Australian Cattle Dog regularly to meet the facility's requirements. It's common for boarding and daycare facilities to require year-round flea and tick prevention to prevent the spread of parasites and disease among their clients.

There are quite a few different flea and tick prevention products on the market, so you'll need to ask your veterinarian to recommend the product that will work best for your dog in the area in which you live. Regardless of brand, most flea and tick prevention medication comes packaged in a plastic vial. The tip of the vial must be broken off so the product can be applied along the back of the dog's neck. You'll need to part the hair on your Australian Cattle Dog's neck so that the medication can be applied directly to his skin, rather than on top of his coat. Be sure to read the accompanying information packet as some products need to absorb into your dog's skin for several days before he can be bathed or allowed to swim. This process will likely need to be repeated every month or so, either year-round or only during warmer months.

Your local pet store or favorite online retailer may also offer a variety of flea and tick collars, but these are not recommended, especially if you have other pets or children at home. Flea and tick collars contain harsh insecticides, such as tetrachlorvinphos, that can cause skin irritation, hair loss, and gastrointestinal distress. In extreme cases, they can also cause seizures or even death. Cats are particularly sensitive to this toxin, so consider other options if you have felines in your home. Tetrachlorvinphos is also considered a carcinogen by the Environmental Protection Agency, so you may be putting your human family members at risk by introducing this chemical into your home.

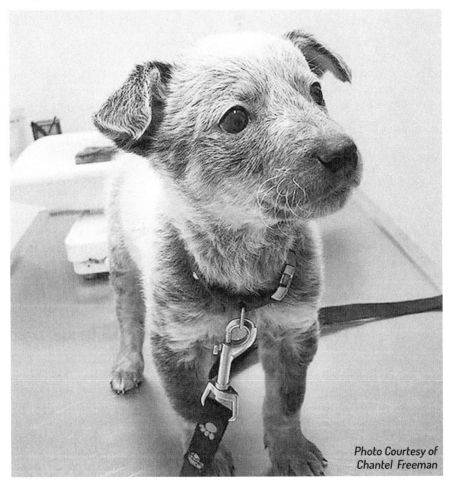

Photo Courtesy of Chantel Freeman

Worms and Parasites

Routine veterinary care is also essential in preventing your Australian Cattle Dog from contracting internal parasites. The exact parasites that may affect your dog vary by area, but your veterinarian will be able to determine which parasites may be infecting your dog and how to treat them. Many internal parasites are zoonotic, meaning they are able to be transmitted to humans, so parasite prevention is crucial in protecting all members of your family.

Photo Courtesy of Stacy Romberger

Although intestinal parasites are most commonly found in puppies, dogs of all ages are at risk. Worms are typically passed from host to host when an animal or human ingests food, water, soil, or feces that are contaminated with eggs or larvae. The most common types of intestinal parasite are roundworms, hookworms, tapeworms, and whipworms. However, worms are not the only parasite that can affect your dog. Protozoa such as giardia and coccidia are also common in most areas. Heartworms are also a common parasite, but they do not infect the digestive track as many other internal parasites. As their name suggests, they are found in the heart and bloodstream. Heartworms are passed from host to host through mosquitos, which transmit the disease as they feed on the blood of animals. Heartworm infections are more difficult to treat than many other types of parasites and can be deadly if left untreated. Treatment often takes several months, and affected dogs must have their activity limited to prevent the dying worms from building up and blocking arteries. Thankfully, heartworms are preventable with a monthly oral tablet, which often also prevents other types of internal parasites.

The most common symptoms of internal parasites include vomiting and diarrhea. Anemia and extreme weight loss are also common signs of a parasite infection. Dogs with particularly heavy parasite loads may also ap-

*Photo Courtesy of
Shantele Rogers*

pear to be malnourished but have a distended stomach. Parasites may also cause dogs to become lethargic or develop a severe cough. It's important to note that many dogs may not show any symptoms at all, so regular testing and deworming is crucial.

Detecting internal parasites is a relatively easy process. A fecal sample is taken and examined under a microscope by a veterinarian or veterinary technician. He or she will be able to detect eggs or larvae in the sample and determine what type of parasite is present so that the right treatment plan can be prescribed. Heartworm testing is a bit different as heartworms reside in the bloodstream rather than the digestive system. A small amount of blood is taken from the dog and is mixed with a chemical solution. This mixture is then placed onto a disposable testing device. After about fifteen minutes, the device will read as either positive or negative for the presence of heartworms.

Treatment for parasites will vary according to the type of worm or protozoa infecting your dog. Some parasites can be treated with a simple oral medication, while others may require injections or a series of medications. Treatment times may also vary, from just a few days to several months. Parasites are easier to prevent than they are to treat, so talk to your veterinarian about the right steps to take in protecting your Australian Cattle Dog.

Holistic Alternatives and Supplements

If you prefer leading a more natural lifestyle, you may want to consider finding a holistic veterinarian. Holistic veterinary medicine treats the animal as a whole, rather than individual parts. For example, if your dog is suffering from arthritis in his hind legs, a holistic veterinarian may choose a combination of nutritional therapy, massage, or even acupuncture to ease your dog's pain. Patients are typically treated using a combination of conventional and alternative medicine. Acute conditions may require surgery or modern medications, while more chronic conditions may be treated with herbal medicine, chiropractic adjustments, nutritional therapy, and acupuncture. Many owners who have difficulty treating their dog's chronic health problems using only conventional veterinary medicine find success using alternative treatments.

If you're interested in finding a holistic veterinarian in your area, visit the American Holistic Veterinary Medical Association's website for a list of approved holistic veterinarians in both the US and Canada. Veterinarians are listed by specialty, species treated, and types of treatment offered.

Vaccinations

To protect your Australian Cattle Dog from communicable diseases, such as rabies and parvovirus, he will need to see a veterinary regularly for immunizations. The immunizations that he will receive can be divided into two categories, core and non-core vaccines. Core vaccines may vary slightly depending on the area in which you live but will generally be the same for all dogs. Non-core vaccines may or may not be necessary, depending on where you live and your dog's lifestyle.

FUN FACT

Angelyne the Amazing DEAF Cattle Dog

Angelyne was born completely deaf, but that hasn't stopped her and her owner/trainer Eric Melvin from giving over 500 inspiring public presentations as advocates for people and animals with disabilities. At her peak Angelyne had learned over 60 cues including hand signals, touch, scent, lights, body language, facial expressions and vibrations. In 2014 Angelyne started going blind, but has continued to perform and amaze crowds to spread her message. Read more about Eric and Angelyne at: www. ericandangelyne.com

Core vaccines are typically given as a combination of antibodies within a single syringe. Sometimes referred to as a five-way vaccine, or DHPP, the most common vaccine protects dogs against distemper, parvovirus, hepatitis, adenovirus cough, and parainfluenza. Veterinarians in some areas may recommend a seven-way vaccine that protects against the previously mentioned diseases as well as leptospirosis and coronavirus. As a puppy, your Australian Cattle Dog will receive a series of three vaccinations, normally at six, twelve, and sixteen weeks of age. As a fully vaccinated adult, your dog will likely need a booster shot every one to three years, depending on your vet's recommendation.

The only vaccine that is required by law is the rabies vaccine, which can legally only be administered by a veterinarian. Rabies vaccines are typically administered to puppies along with their last DHPP vaccine at sixteen weeks of age. After the first rabies vaccines, boosters are typically given every one to three years for adult dogs. Some areas may require your dog to be vaccinated yearly, while others allow veterinarians to recommend boosters every three years.

Non-core vaccines may or may not be necessary, depending on where and how your dog lives. Examples of non-core vaccines include vaccinations against kennel cough, leptospirosis, Lyme disease, and rattlesnake venom. Non-core vaccines typically do not provide long-term protection and must be administered more frequently than core vaccines. They have also been proven to be less effective than core vaccines, so your veterinarian may or may not recommend them, especially if your dog is unlikely to encounter the disease. For example, if you live in an area where rattlesnakes and ticks are not common, it may not be necessary to vaccinate your dog against rattlesnake venom and Lyme disease. Many boarding and daycare facilities require dogs to have been vaccinated against kennel cough before they can stay. Be sure to discuss non-core vaccines with your veterinarian so you can decide if they're appropriate for your Australian Cattle Dog.

Some dogs may experience allergic reactions to vaccines, so it's important to keep a close eye on your dog after any vaccination. Some veterinarians recommend giving only one vaccine at a time to more sensitive dogs to help prevent serious reactions. Symptoms of allergic reactions include vomiting, lethargy, swelling of the face or paws, hives, or swelling at the injection site. More serious reactions may include seizures and difficulty breathing. If your dog begins to exhibit any signs of an allergic reactions take him back to the vet as soon as possible. Many reactions can be life-threatening if left untreated. If you are unsure of your dog's reaction to vaccines, you can always stay in the vicinity of the clinic for 20-30 minutes after vaccinating in case you need to return for treatment.

Titer testing is a new alternative to yearly vaccines that can be helpful with more sensitive dogs. Titer tests measure the antibodies in your Australian Cattle Dog's blood. If the levels are high enough, your dog can be legally exempt from vaccinations. However, if the levels are too low, he will need to be vaccinated again. Titer testing can only be done for core vaccines, as non-core vaccines do not last long enough to warrant testing. To perform the test, your veterinarian will take a sample of blood to submit for testing at an approved laboratory. Be aware that titer testing is often more expensive than yearly vaccinations, but if your dog is prone to allergic reactions, it may be better to test his levels of protection rather than risk his health unnecessarily.

*Photo Courtesy of
Cara Thomas*

Pet Insurance

As the cost of veterinary care rises, many owners may want to consider purchasing insurance for their pets. There are quite a few companies that offer a variety of plans to suit different needs and budgets. You can choose your plan according to the level of coverage as well as the monthly premium. As with human health insurance, premiums may be higher, or coverage may be denied to pets with preexisting conditions.

Unlike your own health insurance, pet insurance typically doesn't cover routine medical care. Regular examinations, vaccinations, and parasite prevention will typically need to be paid for out of your own pocket. There are a few companies that offer coverage for routine care, but they can be expensive. However, in the event of an emergency, such as an accident, or a serious diagnosis, such as cancer, pet insurance can help make treatment more affordable.

Pet owners are divided on whether pet insurance is worth the cost each month. Owners who have had insurance help cover the costs of their pet's treatment are happy to pay the monthly premium, while those who have relatively healthy and accident-free pets may not think that the cost is worth it. Instead of purchasing insurance plans, some owners choose to set aside a small amount of money each month to be available in case of emergency. Before purchasing any insurance plan, it's important to do your research to make sure that you understand the coverage and whether it's right for your situation.

CHAPTER 18

Advanced Australian Cattle Dog Health and Aging Dog Care

Common Diseases and Conditions in Australian Cattle Dogs

"PLL can be an issue. Primary Lens Luxation (PLL) is an inherited disease in some ACD bloodlines. Make sure your Dam and Sire have been tested and cleared. PLL causes the lens suspended within the eye to degrade and break. They can also have Progressive Retinal Atrophy which causes loss of sight until they go completely blind in both eyes. I had a Blue Heeler with this and he lived a good life for six years after he went blind. He even chased a big Labrador out of our yard one evening. He didn't know how big the Lab was, he was blind."

James C Beel
ACD Breeder

Photo Courtesy of
Petra Plank

Photo Courtesy of
Tiffanie Dibble

Although Australian Cattle Dogs are a relatively healthy breed, there are a few conditions that can affect dogs of any age. One of the most common conditions affecting the breed is obesity. Obesity can cause a wide range of health problems but is entirely preventable with proper diet and exercise. Australian Cattle Dogs are also prone to a few orthopedic problems, such as hip and elbow dysplasia, patellar luxation, and osteochondritis dissecans (OCD). These conditions can be genetic or can be caused by injury, poor nutrition, or poor muscle development.

Hip dysplasia is the most common orthopedic condition affecting Australian Cattle Dogs. Dogs with hip dysplasia have abnormally formed hip joints, where the ball and socket of the joints do not fit properly. This improper fit causes the joint to rub or grind instead of sliding as smoothly as in a normally formed joint. The friction causes further degradation of the joint, leading to lameness, pain, and an eventual loss of function. The condition is found most frequently in large and giant breed dogs, but dogs of any size can be affected. Signs of hip dysplasia include decreased activity or range of motion in the hips, lameness, atrophy of the thigh muscles, pain, stiffness, and an unusual gait. Hip dysplasia can be detected by a veterinarian through a physical examination and x-rays. Depending on the severity of the diagnosis, hip dysplasia can be treated with nutritional or physical therapy, anti-inflammatory medications, or surgery. Most cases of hip dysplasia cannot be prevented entirely, but keeping your dog at a healthy weight, feeding him a balanced diet, and providing him with an appropriate level of exercise for his age will help keep his hip joints as healthy as possible.

Elbow dysplasia is similar to hip dysplasia in that the joint is malformed due to nutritional deficiencies, injury, or genetics. The disease is progressive and will eventually lead to a loss of function. Most dogs with elbow dysplasia are diagnosed at a young age, typically after five months of age. Signs of elbow dysplasia include lameness and pain that usually worsens after exercise. Since elbow dysplasia commonly affects both elbows, lameness can be somewhat difficult to detect since the discomfort is symmetrical. However, some dogs will be so uncomfortable that they may refuse to exercise for long periods of time or even move at all. Your veterinarian can detect elbow dysplasia through a physical examination and x-rays. Treatment is like that of hip dysplasia and severe cases may even require a complete joint replacement.

Patellar luxation is a condition affecting the patella, or kneecap, characterized by a dislocation of the patella from the groove within the adjoining bones of the hind legs. The groove in the femur and stifle bones, known as the trochlear groove, is often shallower or malformed in a way that allows the patella to slip out of place. The disease is common in small breeds, but can occur in larger in breeds such as the Australian Cattle Dog. Signs of patellar luxation include a skipping or hopping gait, or the dog periodically moving on three legs. After a few unusual steps, the gait usually returns to normal and the dog may act as if nothing happened. Many dogs learn how to correct the position of the patella with a hopping movement or by extending the leg. Approximately half of all cases of patellar luxation affect both knees. Less severe cases, where the kneecap only occasionally slips out of place, are typically treated with nutritional therapy and are monitored for progression. Severe cases may require surgery to reshape the trochlear groove, relocate the patellar ligament, or tighten the joint capsule to encourage the patella to stay in place.

OCD, or osteochondritis dissecans, is a condition characterized by the abnormal development of cartilage in a joint, most commonly the hock. The diseased cartilage separates from the bone, leading to pain and lameness. OCD is usually caused by nutritional deficiencies, rapid growth, trauma, or genetics. A physical exam and x-rays are needed for a proper diagnosis. Treatment of minor cases may include rest, physical therapy, and nutritional therapy to encourage the cartilage to heal any small tears or cracks. More serious cases, where pieces of cartilage detach and float within the joint, may require surgical repair. As with all orthopedic problems, weight control is essential in preventing excess strain on your Australian Cattle Dog's joints.

Photo Courtesy of
Julie and Marty Hernandez

Genetic Traits Found in Australian Cattle Dogs

"The required testing for this breed for responsible breeding is : Hip Dysplasia, Elbow Dysplasia, An eye exam by an approved Ophthalmologist to observe any abnormalities of the eye, PRA(Progressive Retinal Atrophy), PLL (Primary Lens Luxation), Congenital Deafness, along with the less common but optional testing of PRCD4 and a cardiac evaluation. That is why choosing a responsible breeding who records official health testing with OFA is vital."

Kelsey Bolton
Flintlock Farms

Progressive retinal atrophy (PRA) is a genetic disorder that affects the light sensitive photoreceptor cells of the eye. Over time, the cells deteriorate leading to an eventual complete loss of sight. Early onset PRA is typically diagnosed in puppies between two and three months of age and is sometimes referred to as retinal dysplasia. Late onset PRA is usually diagnosed in adult dogs between three and nine years of age. This disease is inheritable, so affected dogs should be prevented from breeding. Genetic testing is available to encourage responsible breeding practices in affected breeds. PRA is not painful, and the first sign usually detected by owners is night blindness. Affected dogs may act nervous or unsure in dark rooms or at night. In dogs where the disease has progressed more, you may notice your dog acting clumsily, tripping over things, or running into walls, especially in unfamiliar surroundings. Complete vison loss typically occurs after

Photo Courtesy of
Isabelle Dirks

Photo Courtesy of
Dominique Copelin

one to two years, but some dogs may lose their sight more quickly. Unfortunately, there is no treatment for PRA. Antioxidant supplements may help slow cell degeneration but have not been proven to have any effect on the progression of the disease.

Congenital deafness is an inherited condition, so it's important that Australian Cattle Dogs be tested prior to breeding to prevent the trait from being passed on to future generations. The Brainstem Auditory Evoked Response (BAER) test can be performed on puppies as young as 35 days old. Deafness has been found to correlate with certain pigment genes, such as those responsible for piebald and merle coloring in other breeds. The speckled coat pattern of the Australian Cattle Dog has also been found to be connected to congenital deafness. Around three percent of all Australian Cattle Dogs are affected by deafness. No treatment is possible, but many dogs live long and happy lives without hearing. Deaf dogs can be trained to respond to hand signals, but it's important to keep a close watch on affected dogs as they may not be able to hear oncoming cars or other dangers.

Basics of Senior Dog Care

Most experts consider Australian Cattle dogs to be senior at around seven or eight years of age. Of course, this does not mean that your dog will start slowing down on the day of his seventh or eighth birthday. Many dogs begin to display signs of old age much earlier, while others continue acting like puppies for much longer. Australian Cattle Dogs have an estimated lifespan of between 12 and 15 years, so the age at which you begin to notice your dog slowing down may vary. Signs of aging will also depend on your dog's overall health. If he has any serious health problems, he may age more quickly than a relatively healthy and fit dog would.

As your Australian Cattle Dog ages, you may begin to notice changes both in his body and behavior. He may sleep more during the day and you may notice that he gets tired more quickly during walks. After napping, he may seem stiff getting out of bed or he may be reluctant to jump on and off the furniture. Older dogs often experience deteriorating sight and hearing, so you'll need to be more cautious about approaching your dog from behind and letting him run off leash. Some senior dogs may need to go outside more frequently or begin to have accidents in the house. Incontinence is a common sign of aging. Cognitive dysfunction, or dementia, is also common so keep a close eye on your dog if you notice that he begins to act differently or seem confused at times. The most important aspect of caring for geriatric dogs is keeping a close watch on their body condition and behavior and adjust their care accordingly.

FUN FACT
Long Life Span

Australian Cattle Dogs have a long life span for a breed of their size. According to the American Kennel Club, Cattle Dogs have a life expectancy of 12-16 years. That's thanks in part to the fact that they aren't prone to many health conditions.

Grooming

Regardless of your dog's age, regular grooming sessions are essential to his health and well-being. Grooming gives you or a professional groomer the chance to look over your dog's body to notice any changes in his skin or coat, or new lumps and bumps. Some dogs may experience thinning of the coat as they age so you may need to be gentler with brushes and other grooming tools.

One of the most noticeable differences in grooming senior Australian Cattle Dogs is their reduced ability to stand for long periods of time. Your dog may tire more quickly than he used to, so you may need to shorten his grooming sessions. Many grooming professionals choose to work on geriatric dogs for only short periods at a time, allowing them to rest between each session. It's not uncommon for senior dogs to develop cognitive dysfunction, and they may become more aggressive or difficult to work with even if they were well-behaved for the groomer in their youth.

Nutrition

As your Australian Cattle Dog ages, you may need to alter his diet to accommodate his changing body and metabolism. As dogs age, their metabolism slows, reducing their caloric needs. Many senior dog food formulas are lower in calories, allowing the dog to eat enough to feel full while reducing their overall calorie intake. Obesity in older dogs is common, so care must be taken to adjust portion sizes as needed. Excess weight puts unnecessary strain on arthritic joints, which can lead to further immobility.

If your Australian Cattle Dog develops any health concerns in his golden years, you may want to consider supplementing his diet. Joint supplements like glucosamine and chondroitin sulfate can help ease the pain of arthritis. Some older dogs may develop gastrointestinal problems that can be aided with probiotic or fiber supplements. It's not uncommon for older dogs to lose interest in food, so you may need to add tempting toppers to your dog's meals. Adding bone broth or warm water, or even canned food, can encourage picky dogs to eat. Before you add anything to your dog's meals, it's important to discuss your dog's overall health with your veterinarian to make sure the supplements are safe.

Exercise

FUN FACT
Cattle Dogs Age Well

The oldest dog on record is an Australian Cattle Dog named Bluey. Bluey was used as a sheepdog for nearly 20 years before retiring. He lived to be 29 years and five months old.

Aching joints and a slowed metabolism will cause even the most energetic Australian Cattle Dogs to slow down as he reaches his senior years. Not all dogs will begin to show signs of aging at the same time, so it's important to adjust your dog's activity based on his condition rather than the calendar. To encourage your dog to stay as active as possible, it's important to keep a close watch on his weight and make any adjustments to his diet as needed. No matter how old your dog is, he still needs plenty of mental and physical exercise, but it's important not to force him to exercise any longer than he is comfortable.

To accommodate your senior dog's needs, you may need to adjust the way you exercise him. Long flights of stairs or slick floors can be dangerous to older dogs with weakened muscles. Instead of an indoor game of fetch down the hallway, try offering your dog a snuffle mat or puzzle toy filled with kibble or treats. Walking on soft grass may be more comfortable than the hard sidewalk, so consider finding new walking routes. You may find that your Australian Cattle Dog enjoys mental stimulation more than physical as he ages, so it's a great time to try out new activities such as scent work or low-impact trick training.

When It's Time to Say Goodbye

It's never easy to say goodbye to a beloved companion, but the day will come when you need to make a tough decision regarding your treasured Australian Cattle Dog. Remember to reflect on all the joy he gave you throughout his life. Be thankful for the fond memories you have together.

When the time comes to say goodbye, it can be difficult to make the necessary arrangements. It's worth considering your options in advance so that you can be prepared when you need to be. Having a plan will allow you to mourn in peace without having to worry about making arrangements. Many veterinarians offer both in-home and in-office euthanasia services, so talk to your vet about what options you may have. For some owners and dogs, it can be stressful to say goodbye in a sterile exam room, while others would prefer not to have such painful memories of their own home, so do what makes you and your dog most comfortable. What's most important is that you are with your beloved friend to say goodbye. He will be comforted by the fact that his last moments were spent with his loving family members.

When discussing your arrangements with your veterinarian, be sure to ask about your options for your dog's remains. If you would prefer not to deal with such matters yourself, your trusted veterinary team would be happy to take care of the disposal with dignity and respect. Many veterinary clinics also offer cremation and the ashes may be returned to you or disposed of properly. Some clinics also offer a variety of options for urns, or you may take your pet's remains home in a simple box.

Many grieving owners find comfort in creating a memorial for their beloved Australian Cattle Dogs. Memorials can help you remember the good times you shared with your companion and help you through the grieving process. Personalized garden stones, tiles, or other outdoor decorations are an excellent way to memorialize your cherished friend. You may also be able to find ornaments or other decorations that can be made to include your dog's nose or paw prints. There are even companies that can make necklaces or other jewelry from your pet's ashes. No matter how you choose to remember your Australian Cattle Dog, always remember the unconditional love that you shared.

Printed in Great Britain
by Amazon